Dog Training My Way

Dog Training
My Way

BARBARA WOODHOUSE

ᏚᏴ

A SCARBOROUGH BOOK
STEIN AND DAY/*Publishers*/New York

SECOND SCARBOROUGH BOOKS PRINTING 1982

Copyright © 1970 by Barbara Woodhouse
Dog Training My Way was originally published in hardcover in the United
States of America by Stein and Day/ Publishers.
All rights reserved.

Printed in the United States of America
Stein and Day/*Publishers*/Scarborough House, Briarcliff Manor, N.Y. 10510

LC 72-82833
ISBN 0-8128-6082-9

To
all sensible dog owners
who teach their dogs to be
true companions

List of Contents

7

List of Contents

Illustrations

Preface

My first aim, in writing this book, has been to help the one-dog owner. I feel that the average person who buys a dog, and wants it just to be a friend of the family, has very little idea of how to train the dog so that it gives of its best and is a source of joy but never of trouble. This object is generally not acquired without some training. Most people expect the dog to fit immediately into their households although they themselves have not spent any appreciable time on educating it to its new life with them, and then are exasperated when the dog misbehaves. I have used my week-end training courses solely as a basis for giving hints to people to help them overcome individual faults in their dogs' 'way of life'. But I do not think it absolutely essential to attend a training course; this is not the one and only way of learning how to train a dog. This is something anyone, man, woman or child, can do in the home, and in my opinion the home is the right place for the training to be carried out. The main use of a training class is that it gets your dog used to other dogs in large numbers, and this teaches him to ignore dogs in the street and not to fight. A further advantage is that the experienced trainer is there at hand to explain how to overcome particular difficulties. The general training may easily be completed, with the help of this book, at home.

All the individual dogs I have discussed, together with the problems they present, are a composite of many dogs with the same faults; but every day new problems arise and one only learns how to combat them by experience. There can be very few hard and fast rules for training dogs; what will work with one dog might produce revolt in another.

I cannot repeat too often that dogs have, in my opinion, a brain equal to that of a child of about five years old. If spoken to as one would speak to a child, and given a chance to understand, the dog will quickly respond, to the owner's lasting benefit. You wouldn't turn your five-year-old out in the street to amuse itself, hoping for safety; yet this is expected to work for dogs. I believe dog owners shape their dogs' characters according to their own, although I have seen some owners with dogs they don't deserve, and vice versa. You should always bear in mind that the dog picks up your thoughts by an acute telepathic sense, and it is useless to be thinking one thing and saying another; you cannot fool a dog. If you wish to talk to your dog you must do so with your mind and will-power as well as your voice. I communicate my wishes by my voice, my mind, and by the love I have for animals, and by caressing them with my hands. If you are 'in tune' with your dog he will work for you cheerfully and well. Never attempt to train a dog when irritable or angry; you will be sending out waves of irritability which the dog's sensitive nervous system will pick up, and he will worry all the time. Choose a time when you are placid, and looking forward to teaching your dog his useful lessons. Remember sense and sentiment do not always go hand in hand.

Dogs have been faithful friends to man for countless ages, and there is no reason why everyone shouldn't own an obedient companion, but in my opinion it is a privilege to own a dog, a privilege for which one must be ready to make certain sacrifices. We must realize that not everyone likes or tolerates dogs and that if we are devoted to our dogs, and do not wish to leave them behind when going on holiday, the scope of our holiday is thereby limited. We shall have to choose a hotel or lodging house where dogs are allowed, and what is more important, the dog must be so well trained that complaints about it do not arise; if they do, you are creating a precedent which is unfair to other owners of well-behaved dogs.

A holiday abroad is out of the question owing to quarantine regulations. To most of us dog lovers these restrictions are taken as a matter of course. The dog is part of the family, and we wouldn't leave one of the family behind. Some owners are lucky enough to know that their dogs will be happy if provided with good boarding conditions in well-run kennels, and this holiday problem does not exist for them. What does exist for all owners is the risk of the dog getting ill and needing very special care; often the disease produces horrible symptoms and one has to carry out duties which are repulsive; before having a dog you must decide that you are willing to undertake his care 'in sickness and in health'.

Are you willing, too, to prepare his food and see that he gets the right diet, or is he just going to live on anything that comes his way? Most dogs thrive best on regular meals, at regular times, of the correct foods in right proportions. Sometimes it is a nuisance to have to go and buy the dog's food when you are busy, or to have to cook it. Think of this before you become a dog-owner.

Do not listen to people who tell you a big dog cannot thrive in a town or that it is cruel to keep a dog in a flat. A loved dog is happy wherever you live. If he is a loved dog you will see your own living conditions do not deprive him of exercise and a good life. If you have to leave a dog alone in a flat or house all day that is no life for a dog, but no real dog lover would inflict such conditions on his friend. But on the other hand, do not imagine that dogs should never be left alone; a well-trained dog should not require a baby-sitter, but should stay quite happily guarding his owner's property without barking or whining continuously. Many owners complain that their dogs destroy things if left alone; this is a consequence of bad training, and should be firmly checked. An indoor kennel for a small dog makes destruction impossible in the owner's absence, but a big dog must be trained not to destroy. Again, it is the owner's attitude to these things that matters. If he allows a dog to tear and trample things in his presence, and thinks it funny, how can the dog be expected to know that such activity is wrong when the owner is not there? One final question. I am always being asked whether a pedigree dog is easier to train than a mongrel. My answer is that all dogs can be trained if the owner is made of the right stuff. If the owner is at fault, you cannot blame or train the dog. As the ancients say wisely,

> *Have a care o' the' main chance,*
> *And look before you ere you leap;*
> *For as you sow, y' are like to reap.*
> BUTLER

BARBARA WOODHOUSE

1 : Every Owner a Trainer

I feel that in this country there must be few people who have never owned a dog at some time or other in their lives, not necessarily a dog belonging exclusively to themselves, but one shared with the family. The main reasons for owning or sharing a dog come under these three headings in my opinion: for pleasure, profit or protection. I believe by far the greatest number are owned purely and simply for the joy of having a dog either to play with if you are young, or to take for walks and keep you fit if you are not so young, or just for the sheer delight of having a lovely creature round the house to be admired, to admire you, and to keep you company. In this book we are going to exclude those dogs that are kept for profit, as stock-in-trade of a business which must succeed or fail through the amount of money made; the business man or woman presumably sees to it that their dogs are made as attractive as possible to would-be purchasers. If the animals are fierce or illkempt they will not find buyers easily. So we will presume that they are sold before the disobedience, if it exists, has had time to develop or show itself. We are solely concerned with the training and therefore the health of the dog that belongs to the ordinary man in the street.

I wonder how many of these ordinary men in the street give much thought to this matter of owning a dog, before they are attracted by a cuddly puppy, with liquid brown eyes, that begs to join them by their firesides? Very few, I am sure. I am therefore going to try to point out the snags that exist and should be considered before any attempt is made to get a dog. For those who have one already, I suggest skipping a chapter and passing on to later ones concerning the proper training and control of your dog.

First of all, before you buy a dog, decide whether you can afford to give it the home this wonderful friend of man deserves. I don't mean by this that you must be well-off financially to keep a dog. As long as the dog is properly fed, and properly exercised, he is willing to share the humblest abode with his owner. But a dog cannot be kept for nothing. A small dog needs approximately half a pound of meat a day in some form or other, and dog biscuits or brown bread according to its appetite. Therefore I believe that the very lowest sum for which one can keep a dog is a few dollars a week. I know that in some households the dog costs nothing, as there are sufficient scraps from the table to give the dog an adequate and balanced diet, but this is the exception rather than the rule. Next, one has to reckon on the dog licence, and occasionally on the dog getting ill.

One must be prepared, too, to spend a small amount on tonics and on flea powders, and soaps for washing the dog. No dog that is kept in the house should escape a bath or dry clean less than once a month. A good many people say to me, 'How dogs smell! We'd never keep them in the house!' If a dog smells, it is the owner's fault. He wouldn't keep his children unwashed and expect them to remain pleasant companions, yet the dog in some households is expected to keep clean with no help from outside. Have you ever considered how often the dog dips his mouth into gravy, and milk, into meat or fish, and that some of it is bound to adhere to his lips; yet how many people wash their dog's muzzle occasionally? I clean my dog's muzzle very often. But then my dog gets a frequent bath with a really easy-lathering soap. The soap not only cleanses her but protects her from any infestation by insects. However clean you keep your dog, if she goes out for walks in the country she is liable to pick up insects. Bathing also helps to get the old coat out, and the rubbing one gives one's dog in lathering the soap acts as a tonic to the skin.

Another frequent complaint is: 'My dog's breath smells.' Of course it may do, unless you take care to see that your dog eats the right food, that his digestion is in good order, and that his teeth are clean. When one opens some dogs' mouths one is shocked by the state of their teeth. We know that such illness as distemper makes the teeth a bad colour, but a lot of this deposit can be removed if, when the dog is ill, its teeth are kept clean with a piece of rag dipped in salt or some toothpaste. At once we hear cries of 'My dog wouldn't let me open his mouth and do that! He'd bite me!' My answer to that is, 'Why haven't you trained your dog better? What happens when you wish to give your dog medicine?' I suppose there is an awful fuss, much growling, and probably the spilling of the medicine all over the owner's clothes, with the dog breaking away, and much more friction between dog and owner. I believe that dogs should be trained from early days to sit quietly and have their mouths examined, and their teeth rubbed over; and that if any medicine has to be taken, the dog should be told that he must 'come for his medicine'. Then, in spite of the fact that the flavor is nasty, he must learn to take it without biting or struggling. With liquid medicine it is easy, as there is a convenient pouch at the side of the dog's mouth; the liquid can be poured into this, and the dog's head tipped gently, and down it goes (Plate 3). But with pills it is different. With hungry dogs that bolt their food it is easy to wrap a pill in a piece of meat, and down it all goes without the dog knowing it has taken anything; but with a sick dog who doesn't want to eat anyway, one must know the procedure to follow. I always open the dog's mouth and pop the pill right on the back of the tongue (Plate 2). The dog will move its tongue backwards and forwards in an effort to bring the pill back, but if one tilts the head slightly, down goes the pill. In no circumstances should you push the pill down its throat, or one day you will push it down the windpipe, and choke your dog.

If your vet wishes to give an injection the safest thing to do, if your dog is likely to turn round and bite either you or the vet, is to get a handkerchief and tie it round the dog's mouth. Then you should sit on a sofa or the floor and get the dog to lie down with its head in your lap and your arm over its neck. In this manner the dog cannot see what is going on and all is over before he has had time to resent it.

The mental outlook of the owner towards these operations is very important, for the dog at once picks up its owner's nervous reactions; and people who turn a ghastly white when anything has to be done to their dogs are not the ones to hold them for the vet. The dog senses their nervousness and becomes terrified at once. They should try to get a less squeamish member of the family to help. With a very tiny dog, of course, the previous hints do not apply, since one can manage to hold it for an injection with its head turned away from the vet (Plate 1). I never allow my dogs to be injected on the shoulder. If it has previously hurt, the dog fears that everyone who is going to stroke it may be going to give it another prick. If the injection is made in the loose skin just in front of the flank the dog doesn't seem to mind so much, or to have that same desire to bite when being stroked. Fear is one of the most difficult things to overcome in dogs, and that is why we should do everything in our power to prevent anything happening that is likely to leave fear behind. Never let anyone bend down and stroke your dog when it is asleep. It may wake up in a fright and snap without thinking, then it gets a scolding and your dog has a new problem to overcome.

I find one of the most troublesome things to persuade your dog to accept is that he may be caressed in the street by all and sundry. My dog, being a Great Dane, attracts attention wherever she goes. She is just the right height for everyone to stroke without bending down. Therefore, as one cannot stop dog lovers caressing dogs (or baby lovers kissing babies) one has to train the dog to put up with it without showing annoyance or trying to be too friendly. It is always extremely annoying when you have a trained dog, and have put it down to the 'sit' or 'down' outside a shop, to come and find a crowd round it trying to make it get up and talk to them, or trying to feed it on everything from a lollypop to a mince pie. When one's dog is trained fully, it must of course refuse food of all sorts from anyone but its owner or owners. Otherwise there is always the risk that a burglar or some malicious person may poison it. On the other hand there is the risk that a dog so trained, on going to kennels while its owner is away, may refuse food. This has happened and has been extremely worrying for the people concerned. I think if you are likely to leave your dog a lot with strangers, it is best not to teach it to refuse food from other people. I have found occasionally that my dog has had to take food whilst acting in a film, from people other than myself, and I have only had to introduce the person who is to give her food, and tell her it's all right, for her to take the food willingly. But I do not think many of my readers will at this stage have achieved, or perhaps ever will, such perfect communication as I have with my dog. For if they have reached that stage of training they will probably not have bought this book.

One of the vices we are going to tackle are the bad manners of boisterous dogs who jump up on greeting their owners, or visitors to the house, or even people in the street. Other suggestions concern dogs that chew up everything in the house, and which one daren't leave alone a minute in a room without finding there is no longer a newspaper to read, or your slippers to wear. Then there are the dogs who bark incessantly at every one or anything, or the dogs that welcome everyone as though he were a long-lost friend, and won't bark at all (such a one was the dog mentioned in the newspapers recently, who made a bosom pal of the burglar). There are dogs that chase cats or other live-stock; dogs that chase cars and bite postmen; horrid dogs that bite their owners; dogs that are only seen at mealtime, or when they want to be let into the house to sleep. There are the dogs that soil the whole house when they feel like it, and who have therefore to be kept outside for health reasons, as no one should tolerate in the house a dog that is not house-trained. Then there are the dogs that are so clean and well trained that they will not relieve themselves when away from home. I once had a Great Dane like that, and it worried me terribly. I spent one day at the seaside taking her for miles trying to find a suitable piece of grass which she would use. There are the dogs that jump on all the furniture, and refuse to come off. And there are the dogs that steal food, so that one has to be always on the alert not to put a bit of food within their reach. Lastly there are the dogs that won't come when they are called and the dogs that fight all other dogs, so that it is a misery to take them out. We are going to deal with all these misdemeanours of dogs in separate chapters and if in so doing I find myself able to give hints on other problems that crop up as an outcome of these, I shall do so incidentally.

I would like to say that in my opinion if, by the time you have owned a dog six months he has any of the faults I have listed, except nerves, it is in practically every case your own fault. You have not really persisted in training your dog in the right way. I meet an enormous number of dog owners in a year at my courses, and hundreds of others whom I never meet write to me from all over the country for help or advice with the training of their dogs. I am always ready to admit there may be a dog somewhere that is untrainable, but it is a rare exception.

But that is more than I can say of dog owners. There are hundreds of dog owners everywhere who ought never to keep a dog. These are some of the reasons why. They believe that by giving a dog everything it wants it will repay their kindness by implicit obedience and love. That is nonsense. A dog must respect its owner from the day it joins the household. Occasionally in every dog's life there comes a time when firmness is a necessity. If at that time the owner only tries coaxing, the dog will become the master, and the true understanding which exists between the master and dog has been lost. There are plenty of owners who think that it is cruel to control their dog in any way. They really believe that for a dog to be happy it must have complete freedom to go where it will when it will. I have even heard dog owners tell me, not very logically, that it is my duty to put my beloved bitch into kennels when she is in heat so that their dog will not be attracted round to my home when fights and other troubles might develop. The idea that they might control their own dog's movements, and leave my bitch safely in my own home and garden, never enters their heads. To impress their duty on them I have often taken their dogs, unwelcome on my premises, to the police station, and they have had to fetch them and pay for their keep. Another erroneous notion is that a dog is only happy when racing over the countryside chasing rabbits or livestock, and that it must not be thwarted by being called home. The numbers of times I have heard owners telling me it took two hours to catch their dog is unbelievable. These dogs neither love nor respect their owners. A dog that loves its owner cannot bear him or her out of sight or hearing, and will not run off for hours on its own private concerns.

Many owners think a dog should eat until it can eat no more and that it is cruel to give their dogs only the correct amount of food, however much those lovely eyes plead. There are excellent books dealing with the nutrition of dogs, and most dog biscuit manufacturers are only too pleased to tell owners about feeding, so I shall not enlarge on the theme beyond saying that it is not cruel to diet your dog. He will not be too fat, and therefore lazy, when you wish to take him for a long ramble, and lastly he will cost less to keep when given his suitable rations. I do believe that dogs need extra vitamins and that the ordinary diet they get does not always provide all they need. Vitamins A and B are, in my opinion, the ones they seem to need, in most cases, as supplement.

There are thousands of dog owners whose lives are made a misery by their male dogs' insistence on stopping at every lamp-post. This is a thing I never allow. A dog of mine would get his freedom whenever possible and at this time he relieves himself as often as he wishes, but I should get extremely annoyed if I were forcibly stopped by my dog in a walk through the streets, and I should be tempted to commit murder if my dog attempted to relieve himself on a shop front or near anyone's front door. I am revolted by the way dog owners allow this disgusting behaviour. I have dogs brought to my classes who try this one. They are only warned twice and then they are removed from the class. This does not mean that I cannot forgive a puppy or a nervous dog for forgetting himself, it means that an adult dog whose owner is not attending properly to its behaviour, and allows it to soil our hall, will be sent out. Each session only lasts two and a half hours, and any dog can behave itself for that time. If not, the owner is at liberty to take it out for exercise. Most owners think this lamp-post stopping is natural and must be allowed. I wonder whether they do or do not train their children? I look upon dogs, as I have said, as having the same mental capacity as children of five years old, and I think a dog or a child of that age should be trained to cleanliness. And as for dog owners who say that they must put everything out of reach of their dogs, so that it shall not be torn up, and who blame themselves if something does get destroyed because they didn't remember to put it away, I can only assume that they have little else to do. In my busy life, I certainly haven't time to be so careful.

What a joy it is to meet some of the people who train their dogs intelligently and who endeavour, with help, to follow instructions;

who practise their dogs at home, and are rewarded by owning a delightful and obedient pal who can be taken anywhere without a preliminary working-out of the snags. Man's life is made richer by owning a dog, but the enrichment is vastly increased if he owns a well-trained, healthy, clean and intelligent one.

2 : House-Training Your Dog

This is an extremely difficult subject to tackle, as I don't know in what circumstances many dogs have to be trained. But as far as general principles go, I think all dogs must be treated the same way. First, the owner of a new puppy must realize that this puppy has been brought up in a kennel or shed where he had been able to run about and relieve himself at any time, day or night, and it is a great change for him to have to learn to do otherwise. But what does help is that in his new home he is fed at regular intervals, and can't just go and have a drink from his mother at any time. As it is a natural reflex for a puppy to wish to pass water after a feed, this is the first clue to a method of house-training. Always put your puppy out immediately after a meal, and give him the command you will use for ever after. I use the words 'Hurry up', because then no one in the street knows what I am talking about; but it doesn't matter which words you use, so long as in the future your puppy is going to connect those words with his obligations. Immediately the puppy has obeyed your wishes, praise him for all you are worth, then take him in and have a game. Soon after a short gambol, he will feel tired and comfortable after his meal, and he may then safely be put in his basket or kennel, or whatever you are going to keep him in in the house. I strongly recommend all puppy owners to make an indoor kennel. For a small dog an orange box is suitable, with one end boarded up as a bedroom and the other end (where the door is) covered with wire netting or strips of wood so that the puppy has light and air and can see what is going on around him (Plate 4). In his bedroom end must be put a cushion or thick blanket, which he will sleep on; at the other end a turf should be placed, or some peat moss which can be bought cheaply at nurseries, or some sand or earth. Of all these I prefer sand if a turf cannot be obtained. The turf is far and away the best, as then the puppy only connects his 'jobs' with grass, and even in the largest town there is always grass on open spaces. By this method the puppy never soils his bed, but if he cannot wait for his master to take him out he has his grass, which of course must be changed fairly often. I used to find about every two days was enough.

The next question in house training arises when your puppy

wakes up after a long sleep; you must then be ready to rush him out of doors. Most puppies will whimper when they wake up, to show that they are ready for a playtime or a meal. (It is absolutely vital that a young puppy should be kept warm if you want him to become clean quickly; a cold puppy cannot control his bladder.)

Next comes the vexed question as to what one should do when a puppy makes a puddle on the floor. Some people advise rubbing his nose in it. What a wicked idea! Should the puppy make a puddle, catch him, show him what he has done, and scold him resoundingly by your tone of voice, then immediately take him out to his usual spot. This usual spot is another vital chain in the training link. The puppy quickly gets to connect that spot with his 'jobs' and associations are quickly made. If, after puddling the floor, you put him out and he does it again outside, praise him fervently, and with great love in your voice.

The most difficult thing to do is to train your dog to be clean the night through and I sometimes have had my puppy to sleep in my room so that immediately it wakes I rush downstairs with it, and out. I know it's as bad as having to attend to a baby, but I have always had my tiny puppies clean at about nine weeks; in fact, I have twice had six-week-old puppies quite safe to take into hotels with me, with never a mistake. But to achieve this one must always be watching the puppy, and at the slightest sign of sniffing around in an interested manner, must whip the puppy up in one's arms and put him out. Then there is the problem of flat dwellers, probably unable to get up and down stairs quickly enough; the best thing for them to do is to have a large tray or flat box in one corner of the room or landing, filled with earth or whatever you wish to use, and to get the puppy used to going on to that. But of course that does not implant the idea in the puppy's mind that it is wrong to soil in a house. I really feel that if flat dwellers must have a young puppy, they should make the effort to take it out into the street.

Should a puppy ever be smacked for being dirty? I think it should, after the age of six months, providing it has been given every chance to be clean. I have known puppies go out and have a good time and immediately come in and disgrace themselves in the house. That is the time to pick the puppy up and show it what you are smacking it for; give it two or three sound smacks on its rump and put it out again.

Now comes the question of how to keep a puppy warm at night so that it sleeps right through and therefore doesn't wet its box. I always recommend putting puppies in their indoor kennel in the hot cupboard at nights with the door ajar for air. Put a very warm cushion in the box so that when the puppy is lying down the pillow billows up around it much as a litter of other puppies would. A hot bottle is not a good idea. These get cold too soon, and there is always the risk of the bottle getting chewed and the contents soaking the box. If you put the puppy's box by a fire it gets cold towards morning, and a cold puppy is inevitably a dirty, wet puppy.

The other thing that helps a puppy to become clean quickly is to give it its milk or liquid feeds early in the day. Keep the meat or solid feed for the evening meal. I always give the last meal at ten o'clock at night, as dogs have very slow digestions and that meal lasts well round until the morning. I give the last sloppy meal at four o'clock. Be sure to take the puppy out to his favourite spot last thing before you go to bed. We have a tiny black-and-tan miniature terrier which we took on a tour, staying at different hotels each night, and we never had any mistakes with her. We had her blanket and wrapped her up in it at night and put her with the door very slightly ajar in the cupboard usually kept by the bed. It made a snug bed, and I could hear her immediately she woke. If there was a balcony I popped her out on that; if not I went downstairs to the garden. For all these reasons, it is always best to buy a puppy in the summer months: I have never had to house-train one in this way in mid-winter.

The best chance of getting a clean puppy within reasonable time is never to allow him to be free in any room, when very tiny, unless you are there to watch him. Pop him back in his kennel when you have to go out of the room. It teaches him to lie quietly in the one place, and he comes to look upon it as his very own home. A dirty dog in the house is usually a consequence of the owner's just not taking enough trouble to watch the puppy and rush him out quickly. Mothers of children know how essential this watching is; so should dog owners.

Much the most difficult trouble to overcome is the reluctance of a bitch to relieve herself except in her accustomed spot at home. I have never known a male suffer from this particular inhibition, so different is his nature. I have known bitches hold out for well over twelve hours, and it is extremely bad for them. This is where training helps, for if you always use one unvarying word, and expect the bitch to relieve herself when you employ it, she will then know it is not wrong to use the road wherever you and she happen to be. It is usually most difficult when you have a bitch used to using only grass; that is why I advocate also teaching her to use the road. It is all association of words and deed, and this association must be established at a very early age if you are to avoid snags like this. Other

Plate 1. Holding a small dog the correct way for an injection.

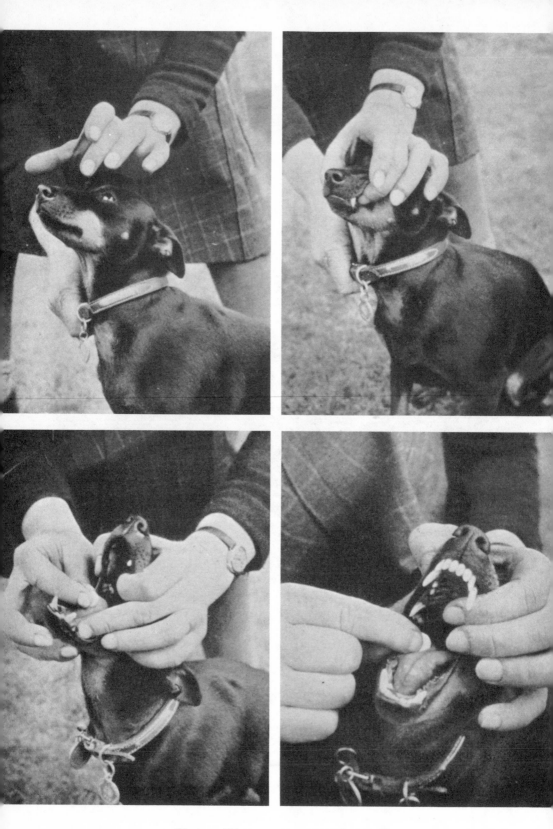

Plate 2. The correct way to give a pill.

Plate 3. How to give liquid medicine.

Plate 4. Housing your dog indoors. (1) An indoor kennel; (2) The next best thing.

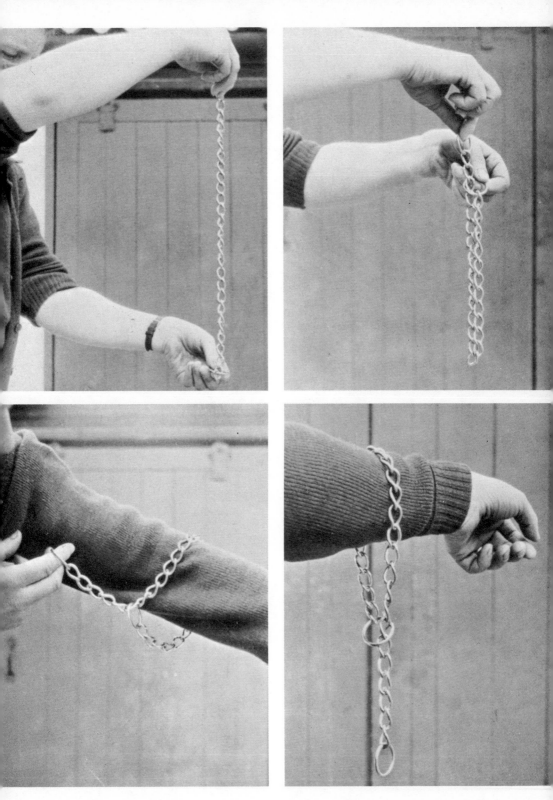

Plate 5. Use of the choke chain. (1) Hold the chain by both rings; (2) Drop the chain through the other ring; (3) Put it on the dog pulling upwards; (4) It automatically loosens when put on correctly.

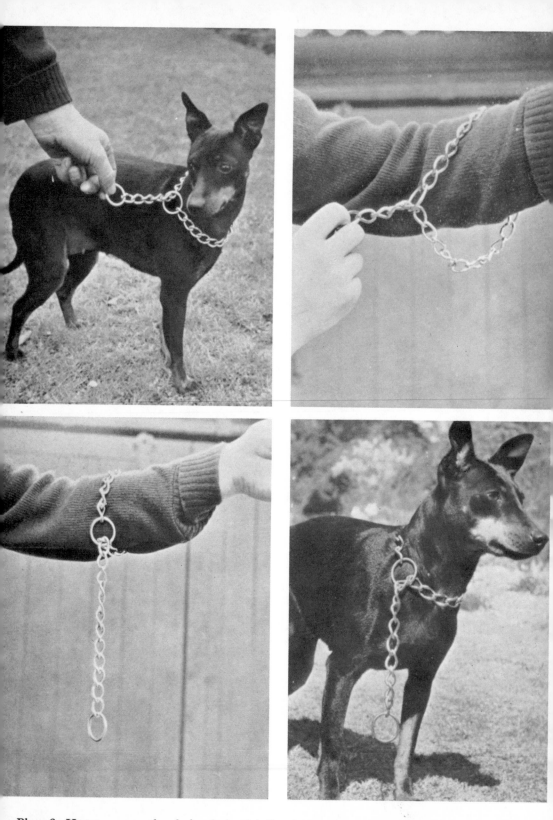

Plate 6. How to put on the choke chain. (1) Correct way to put on a choke chain; (2) Incorrect way; (3) Incorrect way will not loosen itself; (4) Incorrectly put on a dog.

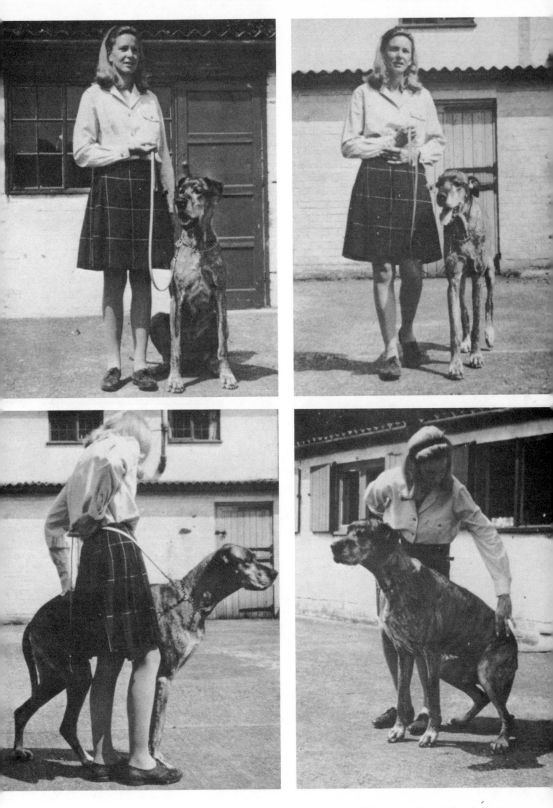

Plate 7. Heel work. (1) The correct length of lead; (2) Walking comfortably; (3) Right hand anchors over hip; (4) Pushing the dog to the sit.

Plate 8. The Recall. (1) Tell your dog to stay; (2) Call your dog; (3) Sit in front; (4) Finish.

Plate 9. Going to heel after recall. (1) After dog has sat in front of you; (2) Pass lead to left hand; (3) Help it to heel with right hand; (4) Pass lead over right hip and make dog sit.

Plate 10. Use of the cord. (1) Put your dog on a cord; (2) Pull the dog towards you.

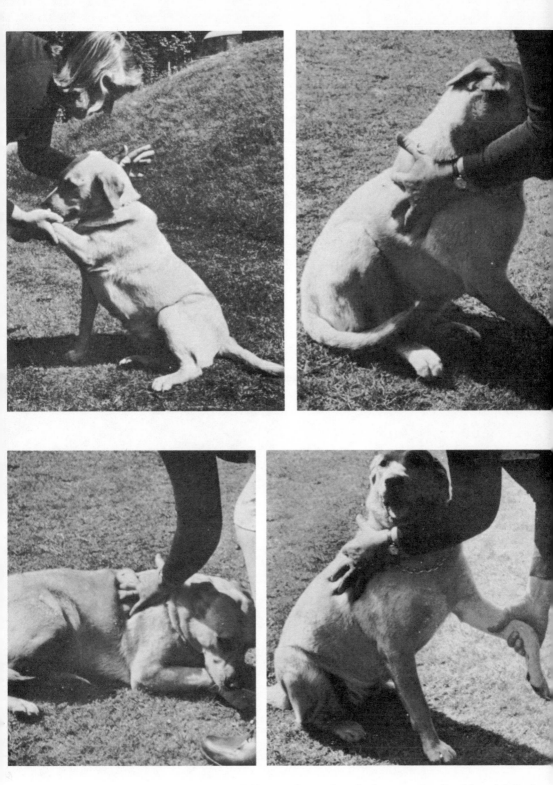

Plate 11. Putting your dog down. (1) Lift front leg and push the opposite shoulder; (2) Push quickly with left hand; (3) Dog lies down; (4) Correct position of hand on dog's shoulder.

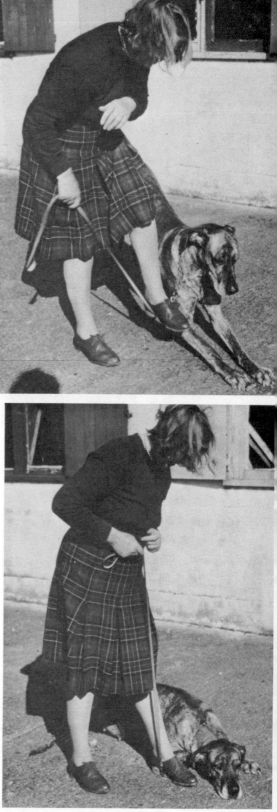

Plate 12. Putting your dog down (*continued*). (1) Place left foot on running end of choke chain, keeping right hand held high; (2) Assert pressure with left foot; (3) Release pressure on choke chain as soon as dog is down.

Plate 13. Advance, stand, sit and down. (1) Leaving the dog at the stand; (2) Sit;
(3) Down; (4) Exercise ends with dog at the sit.

Plate 14. Distant control. (1) Drop hand and give the command 'down'; (2) Raise hand and give the command 'sit'.

Plate 15. Distant control (*continued*). (1) Slap your leg; (2) Give the command 'stand'.

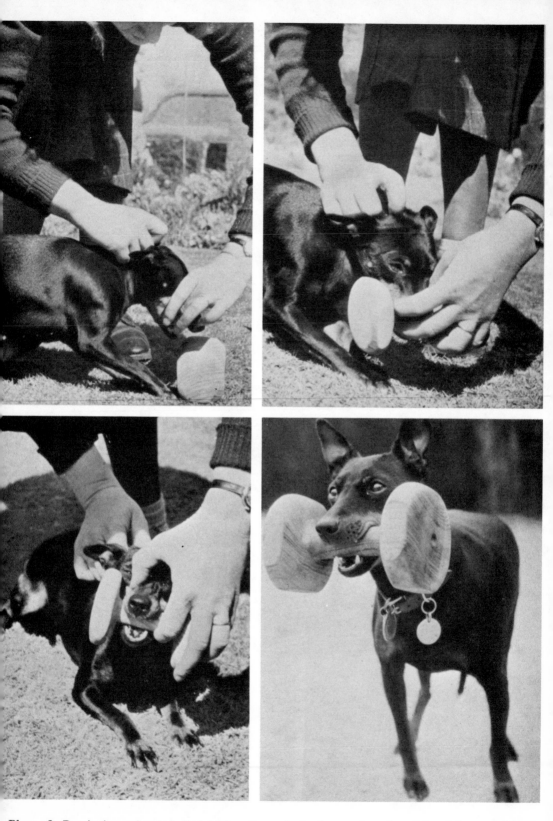

Plate 16. Retrieving a dumb-bell. (1) Place finger in dog's mouth and push head down; (2) Push dumb-bell into mouth with second finger; (3) Allow dog to close its mouth; (4) The finished hold.

considerations apart, it is extremely annoying to have to walk your bitch for a long time, say in rainy or bitter weather, when, had she been taught to behave on command, time and temper could have been saved and the risk of catching cold obviated. I have never known this inhibition occur in kennel dogs, it is usually confined to very clean, house-trained animals.

3 : Early Training for Essentials

'How soon shall I start training my puppy?' is a constant request that I get by letter. I think, contrary to some trainers' ideas, that a puppy is never too young, once it is weaned, to begin understanding small things. I put a very light cat's collar on a very small puppy so that it gets accustomed to wearing something round its neck. It will most likely sit down and scratch vigorously at first, and devote most of the first day to efforts to get rid of it, but harden your heart and pay no attention. If the puppy learns early that it must wear a collar there will be none of that fighting against it later on. Usually the owner gives up in despair and puts on dog straps. One cannot obedience-train a dog on straps, so that is a step backwards. If a dog arrives at my classes with straps I put on a choke chain collar and don't listen at all to the owner's assurance that 'He won't wear a collar'. I don't believe that a dog in good hands should be allowed to have a say in what he will or won't do. The owner must be the judge in every case. If the owner is a fair-minded dog lover he will do nothing that is not right for the dog, unless he does so from ignorance. And there is absolutely no excuse for ignorance on dog management in these days.

Very well then. We have bought an extremely light collar and the puppy has got used to wearing it. What about a lead? A very young puppy should definitely not be taken for walks in the accepted sense of the word. There is a grave risk of infection in the streets, and the puppy gets easily tired; but from about three months old he should have a lead on and be walked about for a short time each day. He is never too young to know that he must come back to your side on the command 'Heel!' But serious training in this heel work should not commence until the puppy is about three and a half months old. It is most important not to allow the puppy to play with or chew his lead. This is an extremely bad habit which is very difficult to break. I had a dog arrive at my class one night that provides a good example of the folly of allowing the lead to become a plaything. Every time his master pulled on the lead, he stood up on his hindlegs and gripped the lead in a vice-like grip with his front paws. That meant one could not pull the lead at all to any good purpose. The only way

26

to break this habit was to pull the dog sharply to the ground whenever he did it. If a puppy learns while walking to play with the lead he never recognizes its authority and just bites it when you wish to give him a jerk. I shall go into the correct methods of training a puppy to walk to heel later.

The puppy is never too young to be taught that when you say 'Bed' or 'Box' or 'Basket' or the name of whatever else you may have as a home for him, you mean that puppy to go to its bed and stay there until you want it. If it gets up to go away it must be firmly put back with the command 'Stay in your bed'. Give him a gentle pat to soothe him before you go away. Naturally the puppy would rather be playing with you or dashing about than staying in his basket, but this training is so very important. All his life there will be times when he must stay quietly in a certain place when you can't have him with you, and it is his early training that matters. If he barks or howls, go back to him and scold him. Never think, 'Poor little puppy, I'll take him on my lap'. If you do, you've lost the first battle. But on the other hand, never leave a puppy too long. Once he has obeyed and stayed quietly in the box for some time, try, if you can manage it, to give him a romp.

I cannot impress on my readers too strongly the necessity to be firm but kind to a puppy. His idea of your authority is forming, and if he knows you give in on the slightest whimper, you are whacked for life. To break him of habits formed when young is far more tiresome than training him in the right way at first. Barking is an inexcusable trick, and if the puppy continues to do it, make sure he is not wanting to go out, make sure he is comfortable and warm, and not hungry. If you're certain on all these points, leave him to yell, only coming back at intervals to speak to him firmly. Then settle him down again quietly and with gentle stroking and words of encouragement, leave him again. Under no circumstances take the dog out of his box when he is yelling, except to make certain all is well. If the puppy thinks he is going to be picked up or let out, you are lost. Usually a puppy will cry for two or three nights at first, on leaving his old home; he misses the warmth and comfort of the rest of the litter or his mother, and his box is a frightening thing to be left alone in. But harden your heart and just try not to listen. Warmth is the all-powerful cure for this sort of thing at night. No puppy can help becoming sleepy in a really warm bed.

The next thing we must stop is the impulse to chew up every thing he sees. This is, or course, a natural thing to do; he is cutting his teeth and he wants to gnaw everything in sight to help his troublesome little teeth through. The answer is, of course, to give him plenty of material that he is allowed to chew. My puppies always have bones in plenty, big marrow bones, not tiny ones that might splinter. A rubber bone is useful, or a hard old dog biscuit, or even an old slipper. Give the puppy plenty to play with, but as soon as he touches something that he mustn't, the firm command and the words 'No, naughty!' must come in. Take the object away and then offer it to him again; if he goes to take it, scold him severely and give the command 'Leave!'; offer it again, and repeat the word 'Leave!'. He will soon know that he mustn't touch that article. The same applies to food stealing. If you can catch him stealing, take the food away and scold him with the same 'Leave!' command. Offer it again, and so on. When you give him his own dinner, give it to him with a lot of praise and always in his own dish. If you use several different plates it is difficult for the dog to know what he may and what he may not take. Teach him to have a piece of meat put between his feet with the command 'Leave!' and then a second or two later pick it up and give it to him with much praise. Anything you give him is right, anything he just takes is wrong. That will help when people offer him things to eat in the street: he will await your permission before taking it.

Do keep to very regular meal times for your puppy. My dogs know the time to a second and I make a point of feeding them (and, incidentally, all my animals) absolutely by the clock. If I happen to be out driving I stop and feed the dog at the right time. I always take their food with me. It keeps their digestions happy, as nature has a peculiar way of making the saliva run and the digestive juices flow ready to digest the meal at those times. I have often seen my dog dribbling at the right time for a meal.

Jumping up is, in my opinion, one of the greatest curses of owning an untrained dog. With a puppy, one is inclined to forgive it as just a show of exuberance, but later on, when the dog comes in with muddy paws and jumps up for play, or a kiss, it can be the ruination of a dress or suit. Therefore stop this trick in the beginning. I always kneel down when really praising a small dog, so that the inclination to jump up needn't arise. The dog only jumps up to be near your face. Faces have a fascination for dogs. A well-trained dog never takes his eyes off his master while working in a competition, and this eagerness to be near his master's face begins very early in life.

Quite often I am asked: "Am I likely to catch any disease if I kiss my dog?" I always reply that only one ill is communicable to man from dogs and that is the tapeworm, so if you want to kiss your dog don't kiss his nose or muzzle. I always lay my face against a dog's cheek so that I can whisper sweet nothings into its ear. I have trained our little English Toy Terrier to wait for a kiss; she puts her head on one side and waits until I give her a kiss before showing terrific pleasure by really lifting up her upper lip in a toothy smile. Sometimes I have to give her five or six kisses before she is satisfied: I really have to love her a lot! Dogs adore affection. I know very few owners who really give their dogs all the affection they need. Of course there are cranks who overdo it but we are not concerned with such people, who probably lack love in their normal human relations and who therefore give exaggerated affection to their dogs and expect it to be returned. One must have a reasonable perspective in these matters.

I believe it is essential to talk to your dog as frequently as you would to a child. You will be amazed how much your dog understands, not only by the tone of your voice but from actual words. I save myself many an unnecessary journey by asking my dog to go and 'shut the door' or 'fetch the newspaper', etc. I have no trouble at all in teaching her a new thing to do, because she knows so many basic words, as for example, 'go', 'fetch', 'bring', 'put it over there', 'come', 'sit', 'stay', 'down', 'away', 'corner', 'go round', 'turn round', 'walk back', etc.; in fact, there are a vast number of combinations of words in a dog's dictionary. It is your business to help him build up this vocabulary, beginning with his name, then simple words like the 'Box!' 'Leave!' and 'Naughty!' already mentioned, then perhaps 'Bone', 'Dinner', and the various names of objects or actions that fill him with pleasure or excitement. As his comprehension of single words grows, so does his power of understanding separate sounds strung together.

Now we have covered several important aspects of early training: we have trained our dog to be clean in the house; and to stay quietly wherever his box is; and to refrain from stealing food. We come now to the vexed question of how much encouragement he should get to bark at the telephone or at the doorbell, of how to teach him to stop barking or start barking. It is quite easy to teach him to bark by getting someone to bang on the door, whereupon you rush towards it with tremendous excitement, 'barking' yourself and getting terrifically worked up. The dog soon understands this game and should learn in under an hour what he is supposed to do. The greater trouble comes when you want to stop him. As he barks, you go to the door and open it. If it is a friend, you tell the dog 'That will do' and if he doesn't stop barking immediately, scold him and straightaway put him, lying down, into his kennel. He will soon come to connect the words 'That will do' with being put in his kennel, or down, and as you say 'That will do' he will soon learn to stop barking in anticipation of being put in his box. He also connects the words with a scolding. But always remember to praise him, when he barks at first with 'Good boy!' then follow it by 'That will do' and the command to go and lie down. Few dogs bark much when lying down.

Some dogs bark for hours if left alone in the house. The reason for this is loneliness, and the barking is really a compliment to the owner. But it is also a vice, and must be stopped. The only way to stop it is to train your dog while you are in the house to be put in another room with its blanket or basket, and to stay there quietly. At first it will bark very loudly. The owner must return very crossly and send him to his basket with extremely angry words. The dog will try to fawn over the owner, but under no circumstances must one give in. When you have got him lying down, change your tone of voice to a soft soothing one, and with plenty of praise tell him to 'stay, there's a good boy', leaving him in a slow comforting manner. If the dog is quiet for about half an hour go back and praise him with all the fervour you can muster, let him romp about, and take him with you to your sittingroom or wherever you are; show him that you think he is the cleverest and most wonderful dog you know. If you do this daily your dog will learn that you are coming back and will eventually lie down quietly wherever you put him. But this is not taught in a day, and is never taught at all by a weak-willed owner. I maintain that to train a dog successfully the owner must be absolutely determined that with kindness and firmness he will make the dog do as it is told. The dog must get the impression that if he doesn't do right there is going to be real trouble with him, but if he does do right he's going to have a wonderful time.

I think you will find that a dog that has been trained to stay anywhere quietly in a house will also stay happily in the street in your car. I often think a dog is best left in a car rather than outside a shop, although I am often shocked by the way owners shut the windows up tight in hot weather until the dog is really suffering. One's dog should be so trained that if the windows are all open a few inches he will not try to get out. At first, give him his own blanket or cushion on the back seat, so that he has the comfort of familiar things around him. He should bark if a stranger comes too close to the car he is guarding. It is natural for any dog to guard its owner's property. Should the dog lack the guarding instinct, it must be taught, with the help of a friend. Get the friend to approach the car and as she puts her hand on the door, tell your dog in a rousing voice to 'see her off' or 'bite her'. This must be said with so much vehemence that the dog is egged on to such a state of excitement that he naturally barks. Directly he does so, praise him, and repeat this as often as is necessary for the dog to get to know that guarding is his job. To bite is only taught when the stranger has protective clothing on, and I think the average car and dog owner will be satisfied with a barking dog in a car. Training to bite is a risky undertaking; the training of guard dogs is a specialist job, and the ordinary dog owner should be wary of training his dog to do more than bark fiercely and agitatedly. Once a dog has been taught fierceness, the lessons are extremely difficult to unlearn.

I get many letters from dog owners whose dogs tear the edges of their husbands' trousers or overcoats; in fact they tear the clothing of anyone who comes to the house. The quickest cure I know for this is to arrive at the house and go straight to the kitchen, fill a small jug, walk on, and when the dog starts tearing, to pour some water over its head. The dog gets such a shock that it doesn't often do it again. This method is better than all the scolding in the world, for the dog doesn't know where the water comes from, he only comes to realize that cloth-tearing causes it to flow.

Dogs that kill chickens have so often been put to sleep as incurable that I hasten to tell readers of a cure I have never known to fail. It means slaughtering another chicken, but it is worth it. Get the dog on a very long cord, about twenty feet in length; if it is of string he won't notice he has it on. Then catch and kill a chicken, and while it is fluttering as they do after death, throw it down away from you. The dog will immediately rush in to the kill. Pull him sharply by the cord, pick up the chicken and hit the dog everywhere with it. The feathers will go all over his face, he will try to escape, but you have him on a cord. Keep on for ten seconds, not hitting him hard enough to injure him, as the secret of the cure is the fright he gets when the chicken attacks him instead of letting him kill it. Next throw the chicken down away from him and loose the cord. If he shows the slightest indication of going after it, repeat the performance, but hit a good deal harder this time. I have never seen a dog need this treatment more than twice. The old trick of hanging a dead chicken round the dog's neck has no effect at all.

I had an urgent 'phone call from a lady the other day, telling me that her dog had taken possession of her bed, and neither she nor her husband could get it out, as it bit them on their approach. This is a common trouble; perhaps the dog may take the best chair and refuse to get off. The owner perhaps gives in the first time, from laziness or fear, so the dog does it again. But when you wish to go to bed and can't, because the dog says no, things have become serious. I went to the rescue of the couple I am talking about, and for me it was extremely annoying, for the dog immediately sensed that here was the sort of person who would tolerate no nonsense, and immediately came out of the bed wiggly-waggly fashion, doing his best to show me what a really delightful person he was by licking my face, and showing great friendliness. I told the owner to put him back in the bed while I went outside, but the dog knew that this was not the moment for repeating his act, and allowed his mistress to remove him from the bed without making any kind of protest. The cure which the owner should have adopted was to have put on thick gloves and an overcoat, grabbed the dog by the scruff of its neck, shaken it vigorously, and allowed any bite to come to nothing on thick cloth or leather. Always have a long piece of string on the dog collar so it can be pulled off the bed or chair by the string.

I asked what other tricks this delightful creature could produce, and was told that he was very fond of snatching and stealing food; and if anyone tried to take it away he would bite. So I got her to fetch a piece of meat and the dog promptly snatched some. I took the meat, and just as the animal was going to seize it I said 'Leave!' in a thunderous tone. The dog sat back astonished, I offered it the meat again, and repeated 'Leave!' in an ordinary tone; the dog did not attempt to touch it. Next I gave it to the dog with great praise and gentle coaxing. He enjoyed it. Now came the real test, which was to take the meat from the dog when actually in its mouth. I gave it a large lump which I knew it would have to chew, and directly it had the meat in its mouth I said 'Leave!', again in a very fierce voice. The dog stopped chewing and I opened its mouth and took the meat away. I then gave it back, with much praise. I consider that a well-trained dog should drop what it is eating immediately on command. I have taught my dog, by these means, never to eat a rabbit bone. I take all the bones I can see out of the rabbit she has, but I do miss an occasional one. I always watch her eating and as soon as I hear a bone crunched, I tell her to drop it. The food is immediately dropped from her mouth and I remove the bone. After a short while she realized that it was the bone I wanted, not the food, and now if she cracks a bone she instantly drops it out on the plate and very carefully picks the food away from it. In the same way, I can give her a mutton bone and tell her to eat it as long as it doesn't splinter. Immediately it cracks she drops it and won't touch it again until I have examined it for safety.

The cure for all biting dogs that sharpen their teeth on their owners begins with protection for the owner; then, as he knows he is certain not to get his hand bitten, he can go over to the attack, and the biting dog gets what he didn't bargain for. I have advocated a loose muzzle before now and ordered the dog to do my bidding; he has at once gone to bite, forgetting he is muzzled, then I scold him very severely and force him to do what I want at least three or four times in succession, knowing he can't hurt me. I have never found this method to fail. Owners have found it to fail as they hate doing such things to their dog, but you are driven to use severe measures with a bad dog. It is probably the owner's fault in the first place for allowing the dog to begin a vicious trick. I have always found that men's thick leather gloves, and a man's overcoat that reaches over my hand a bit, give complete protection against any dog, although only about four dogs in my life experience have tried to bite me; they do what I want them to, 'or else', as the saying goes, and well they know it. Yet the funny thing is that they love me for it. The naughtiest dogs and I have a great love for each other, and some of the cured ones won't rest in my class until I have loved and kissed them. To me they are the most precious of all. When I am brought really naughty dogs it is a challenge to my love for them, and I never feel happy until they are well behaved and have regained their faith in human nature; for that is what they have lost, or they wouldn't be so wicked.

Some owners have constant trouble on their hands because their dogs persist in chasing cats or farm animals. In most cases, I think it is the owner's own fault. They possibly don't like cats coming into their gardens from the houses next door and have themselves chased the cat out. The dog has seen this, and noticed the angry and yet rather thrilling tone of his master's voice, and thinks this is a grand game. Possibly the owner doesn't bar the dog from coming when he goes after the intruder. How can you expect the dog to know that it is wrong to chase a cat, when Master does it? The habit may not arise in this way; it may be just the dog's natural instinct to chase anything that runs before it. If the inclination is checked early enough by simple scolding, it may leave the dog for ever. But if it has been left too late for this, once more our old friend the long cord must come into use. The dog should be taken out and allowed to run as freely as possible on the cord. If he starts chasing anything, jerk him sharply on the cord and scold him; then free him again. Next time he does it, smack him. He will begin to understand that chasing things isn't such fun as he thought. My way of teaching my dogs not to chase anything is to find our cat and tell the dogs to 'talk to the lovely pussy'. I use a most endearing note, showing them that I adore the cat and they must love it too. My Dane several times collected for the blind at Championship cat shows and was photographed with the cats either in their big cages or playing happily between her paws. I hate to see animals unfriendly to each other. One of the loveliest sights at my home was to see my Dane licking the face of a new-born calf. They were always her special care, as if she hoped to make up to them for the loss of their mother.

I think I should conclude with a few more references to this very annoying habit dogs have of jumping up. I have suggested that one should always kneel down to speak to them, but this won't stop a confirmed 'jumper-up'. There are two ways to treat him; the first we hope will be successful, but, if not, the second is bound to be. The first way is this. When your dog rushes at you and jumps up, grab him quickly by the collar and say 'No, naughty, sit!', at the same time holding him by the collar (close to the neck, immediately under the chin) and pulling him down to the sit. Then when he is down in that position, praise him tremendously, doing this, if you can, while kneeling on one knee, so that he feels you are his own size. The other is the harsh way, which of course may have to be used, and that is a slap on the nose with the command 'Down!' Some people suggest using a newspaper to do this with, but I don't agree. The dog can easily catch hold of the newspaper and think it is a game. Don't forget the praise as soon as he is lying or sitting down instead of jumping up. After all, this jumping up is only his way of showing his owner he loves him dearly.

The last point in this survey of preliminary training is of more interest to housewives than to the man owner. If you train your dog to wait at the house door for permission to go in, you will always be able to wipe his feet after a muddy walk, and so spare your carpets. Other aspects of 'Waiting on Command' are dealt with in Chapter 9.

4 : More Advanced Training

Your puppy has now reached the age when you consider he is getting big and boisterous and you think he should be taught to walk correctly to heel. He should learn to do this with or without a lead, for even if you come only occasionally in contact with traffic it is never wise to have a dog on the road without a lead. In towns, of course, a lead is a 'must'. Some people with beautifully trained dogs like to show them off without leads. They will do so until one day something quite unexpected happens and the dog is frightened into the road and causes an accident. In England, for instance, 70,000 accidents on the road every year are caused by dogs, 3,000 of these accidents actually causing human casualties. I feel sure that readers of this book would not wish their dogs to kill or be killed on the road, and the first precaution to take (except in the country or an open space) is to keep the dog on the lead.

To the ordinary dog owner, keeping a dog on the lead means a tiring process of being dragged along at the dog's pace, having to talk to every other dog one meets, having to sniff at every corner, and generally being at the mercy of the dog. To me it means that my dog will walk quietly to heel without paying attention to any other dog, and when I increase speed my dog will do likewise; or should I wish to shop-gaze, my dog will dawdle too. Should I wish to stop and chat with a friend, my dog will sit and wait patiently without command. In fact I want to know I have my dog with me without being uncomfortably reminded of the fact. To get a dog to this stage of training takes time and patience, but it is possible for everyone who accepts that the essentials are great patience, great love of your dog, above all the will-power and determination to succeed. There are many methods of training a dog, and I don't claim that mine are the only successful ones. I train a great number of dogs in the shortest possible time, as it is a work I love, and quick results mean I can help more dogs. Everything written in this book has been tried out in many, many cases and proved helpful, but I am learning new and extremely useful procedures all the time. For example, I was having great trouble the other day in the matter of teaching a dog to fetch its dumb-bell. It would do so cheerfully for me, because I sounded enthusiastic, but its owner is very shy and she could not easily get that note of excited expectancy into her voice. I noticed the joy with which the dog leapt about after having done the exercise well, and in my own excitement I gave it a little clap. So next time I asked the owner to try, I clapped as she gave the command; away went the dog with evident happiness, connecting my natural exuberant clapping with the fun of fetching a dumb-bell; so I had discovered another little device for helping the nervous.

Another dog would not sit straight in front of its owner when called. So I got a few helpers and we made a line on either side of the owner, so that the dog had to come up the passage and sit straight. Slowly we widened out, and the dog still sat straight; simple when you know how, isn't it?

So many dogs scream the place down hysterically when told to lie down, or when doing something necessary they don't want to do. It is extremely hard for the owners not to give in immediately, chiefly so as to stop the noise, in case the neighbours might think they were being cruel. The truth is it is cruel to give in, for the dog has then allowed its nerves to get the better of it. Shut your ears and go on compelling the dog to do what you want, praising and stroking encouragingly all the time; repeat the exercise three or four times with a lot of caressing in between, and you will have done much to make the dog get over its hysteria.

You would imagine that attendance at a class, with all the noise and bustle, would be the very last way to cure a nervous dog; but it works out otherwise. The reason is that there is so much going on all round it that the dog doesn't know what, specifically, to be frightened of, and soon pays no attention to hurrying feet or bounding dogs. I had two adorable show Pekes the other day who wouldn't hold their tails up in the show ring and were thus losing the prize cards. I suggested that they just come and stand in the middle of the room with all the dogs going round. I took them there, and in a happy cheerful, voice encouraged them to come for a romp. In no time, up went their tails, and I hope they will now win the much-sought-after prizes.

Dogs suffer from inhibitions and fears we do not understand. They are waiting for a lead from their owner, and if the owner can transmit to them his confidence in them, that is half the battle. I hear so many people say, 'I know my dog won't do this or that'. I reply, 'You mean that you know your dog *will* do it, if you know how to instruct it'; and that is the secret, mutual trust and belief. It means you must train yourself before you can train your dog. If you have no confidence in yourself, your dog knows it.

Therefore I suggest that before you start to train a dog, you should read as much as you can about the efforts of other trainers, if possible see how it is done, then go and do your best to carry out all the exercises, convinced that success is not far off.

5 : Training to 'Heel' and 'Sit'

So much, for now, for puppy rearing. Now I am going to suppose that you have acquired a completely untrained dog of three and a half months or over. The age doesn't matter. Time and time again I am asked, 'Is my dog to old to train at three years or more?' I answer, 'that the age of the dog, providing it is not too young, does not matter. I have trained dogs at eight years old, and many times trained them at five and six years old.' Far more important than the age of the dog is the disposition of the owner. I am going to give a few examples of owners I have met and if you fall into one or another category I hope you are either duly proud or duly ashamed of yourself.

The first owner arrives usually with a medium-sized or small dog. The dog is shown to me as being quite impossible to train, as probably having been taken to the vet for pills to quieten it down, but all to no effect. I am, I am told, its owner's last hope. The owner is usually a very excitable person, as often as not a woman. Her nervous speech and movements and constant chatter make me realize at once that the dog is only copying its owner when it displays symptoms of hysteria. It fights other dogs because its owner inevitably gathers it up in her arms or shortens its lead to choking point on approaching another dog, so that the dog at once stiffens and expects a fuss when he sees another dog in the distance. This owner has got to learn that her dog is a good dog if only it is given the chance. I usually take it from her and demonstrate that the dog doesn't attempt to attack other dogs if I take it along with me. I have to make her understand that to train the dog she must believe that she can make it behave and it is not witchcraft on my part when the dog behaves with me.

The next type of owner is a very nervous type of man or woman, usually elderly, with a large animal that is far beyond their strength. He or she literally hasn't the physical power to give the dog the sharp jerks on his choke collar that are the preliminary to all good heel work. I tell them I think the dog is too much for them, but they insist that they adore big dogs, and 'he's such a darling' if he wouldn't pull them over, steal their dinner, go off alone most of the day and chase everything that moves. Again it is usually I that have to give this dog its first lesson in the meaning of a choke chain collar, in fact I have nearly to choke him before he finally realizes that it is far more comfortable to keep to heel on a loose lead than to pull on a collar that tightens round his neck as he pulls.

The next type of owner is the one who arrives with the tiniest toy dog, complete with cushion, and does so want the dog to behave but it is so tiny to teach anything to. I adore training these mites, and have, in my time, spent many hours on the floor coaxing one of them to retrieve a dumb-bell. I have before now given a sharp slap to a tiny miniature Dachshund who with malice aforethought defied my every command. I have used two fingers only, and been most careful to smack in the right place. Some of these little mites can be extremely stubborn and no amount of coaxing will alter their behaviour.

Horror-struck onlookers have wondered how I could do such a thing, but I always maintain that I am the best judge of what to do with a dog. Had the owner been the best judge, it would not have been necessary to attend classes. In every case I punish a dog without feeling angry with it, and then only after every other means has been tried.

While I am on this matter of smacking dogs, I should like to pass on what I hear from many owners on their methods of punishing their dogs. When the dog is caught in the act of doing something dreadful the owners have several ways of showing their displeasure. Quite often, people tell me: "Oh, I don't speak to my dog all day.' Can you imagine any dog seeing the point of this? If that is a sensible punishment, then I suppose we are to keep up a constant chatter to our dogs in order that they may understand that we are pleased with them! It sometimes happens that I do not speak much to my dogs in the course of a day; they quite understand, then, that I am very busy or worried. The other night I was both busy and worried and it wasn't until my husband said, 'Look at your dogs, Missis,' that I glanced at them and saw they were both lying gazing at me, their eyes full of urgent entreaties to go and get their dinner. Both tails were wagging and both heads were lying between their paws. They were relying on their beautiful eyes, that were fixing me with a stare, to make me understand what they wanted, without barking or disturbing my train of thought. Those dogs didn't take my silence as a punishment, but they knew I had temporarily forgotten them. I believe they thought that by concentration and telepathy they would attract my attention: as they would have, before long.

Another type of owner scolds her dog in the most gentle manner possible, being quite certain in her own mind that harsh words may cause severe and permanent injury to her dog. I fear that as a punishment for stealing or biting, or some such deed, this type of mild rebuke will get you nowhere. If your dog is as sensitive as this, one look from your displeased face will send him to the corner in a misery. I believe that if your dog really loves you, and you him, a bond exists between you, so that your merest hint of crossness is conveyed to him without words being said. But I maintain that if you have created that bond, you won't be at training classes.

The next type of owner gives a sound thrashing for whatever wrong the dog has done, believing the theory that 'the more you beat them the better they be'. This just gets a dog muddled and very unhappy. Some dogs cringe and show every kind of allegiance to this kind of behaviour, and I often think that the animals that do the best heel work clinging to the sides of their handlers in obedience tests, have had one or two beatings before this level of obedience is attained. I would any day rather see an animal walk quietly to heel in an easy manner than cling in terror to the legs of its owner. But then I do not really approve of the artifical manner of working dogs in these tests. To my mind, it almost amounts to mental cruelty to expect it to work with certain dogs.

To resume: I think experience shows that if by a quick smack you can cut short the nagging necessary to make a dog do something which it is quite imperative he should do, then give a quick smack when you are not in a temper, and immediately show that you bear no malice. Recently it was so cold that instead of having a training class in our Nissen Hut I invited the handlers and dogs into my drawing-room and rolled back the carpets. This meant that we had a very confined space, and if we were to gain any benefit from a class under these circumstances the dogs not working at any given moment must be kept lying down and quiet. This was a good exercise in itself. One young poodle would not lie down; he would sit, but while sitting kept up a ceaseless, stupid whimper.

I gave the owner instructions as to how to put him down, but the poodle won every time by getting up again. The dog owner had had every chance to show how the dog would behave, and as the animal was spoiling the class for the rest of the handlers I went over, gave a firm command and the lightest of slaps on his lordship's posterior. He lay down at once, put his head between his paws, and went to sleep. He knew I meant what I said and certainly *felt* I meant it. When I was ready to have him work I went over to him in a very pleasant manner, and spoke to him amiably; he was delighted to see me, and we had both forgotten the former incident. I need not have slapped him. Had I had time to reason with him I could have made him do exactly what I wanted with nothing but my voice, but in class one hasn't always the time to give the necessary individual attention to each misbehaving dog. I believe the smacking of dogs should not, as a rule, be done by the owners. If the dog is behaving badly enough to require punishment the owner is probably in a temper, and I don't think anyone should hit in a temper. One inevitably regrets it. If a trainer does it in a calm way, without temper, the dog understands what it is all about.

In all future descriptions of how to train your dog I shall leave out all reference to corporal punishment. It is a very distasteful subject to all dog lovers. I have given my views as to the occasions on which it seems reasonable for a dog to be punished in that way, and I shall always think a dog caught in the act of doing something quite unpardonable is more quickly taught there and then by a sharp slap than by all the talking to in the world. If you need to smack your dog, in my opinion you have failed, as a trainer, to exert proper influence on him from the beginning. That is why your dog has to be broken of his bad habits the hard way.

Most people come to my courses in the right spirit, realizing that to train perhaps twelve dogs and handlers in a total of six and a half hours needs an almost super-human effort on my part; that is, if I am not content just to stand in the middle of a class and yell orders. My idea of training is that all the dogs should learn properly exactly what I set out to teach them, and I am afraid I spend a long time sometimes on a particularly difficult dog, trusting that the other members of my class will forgive the time filched from their own charges. I remember one day I was having tremendous trouble with a little toy dog and her dumb-bell; she just would not leave her mistress to go and pick it up, although if I took her and put it in her mouth she would run happily back with it. I sat on the floor and spoke to her in my 'little voice' and kissed her unashamedly; quite quietly I gave her confidence through my own love for her, and presently up she got and trotted off to fetch her dumb-bell. A few weeks after that she won a prize in a Special Novice obedience test at a championship show. Without that time spent on her, she would never have done it. It was typical of the spirit of the other dog handlers that immediately this little dog did the exercise in the class, there was a spontaneous outburst of applause. We all so want the dogs to work well, that you could hear a pin drop sometimes when I am having a particularly tough time with a dog. I often feel that everyone is willing me to win, and persuade the dog to behave well.

I find this training of dogs the most fascinating work possible. Sometimes it breaks my heart to see the utterly unsuitable owners

that intelligent dogs have to put up with. Often I have to train the
dog in spite of its owner. Some dogs I know will never be trained
after they leave me. Whatever we do in the class is left unpractised
directly the class is over. I think some members come for an enter-
taining weekend, but to those who come and really make progress I
always feel extremely grateful. For by the mere fact of having a
well-behaved dog on the streets they are helping to spread the gospel
that training pays all along the line.

The first exercise must be to train a dog to walk nicely on and off
the lead. First you require a choke chain of the required length and
type. The thin small links on some that are on the market are quite
useless for training a dog kindly. The broader the link the less
likelihood of any damage to the dog's coat, and one can get more
purchase on the dog with a broad chain than a narrow one. Lengths
of these chains vary. Small dogs need sixteen to eighteen inch
lengths. Bigger ones, up to twenty-eight inches. Tiny tots need the
finer and smaller chains still, although I consider that a very small
dog need not have a choke chain at all. Next, you take hold of both
rings at each end in different hands, and with one hand held high
above the other slowly drop through the lower ring, until both rings
meet each other (see Plates 5 and 6). I once sent a man a choke chain
through the post and it came back twice with the remark that he was
not a conjuror—the rings wouldn't go through themselves as they
were both the same size. The rings do not thread through each other,
but the chain is dropped back through one ring. Now that the chain
is correctly threaded, put it on your dog so that the chain pulls in an
upward direction when on the dog's neck; in this way the chain
immediately loosens when you release the pull on the lead. If you
put the chain on so that it pulls downwards when on the dog, it does
not free itself but stays tight even though your lead is loose. This
means that you are punishing your dog when he should not be
punished, and spoils the whole idea of letting your dog realize that as
soon as he stops pulling he is quickly comfortable again. This choke
chain is in no way cruel; the only effect it has on the dog is it quickly
gives up the idea of pulling and becomes a nicely behaved animal.
Now that you have presumably attached your choke chain in the
right manner, the correct length of chain should be such that when
threaded through itself it has a couple of inches of so loose to spare;
that means that it is easily put on over the dog's head. Never try to
force on too small a choke chain for this could hurt or frighten the
dog.

Next, the lead must be fixed to that ring of the chain that is doing
the pulling upwards. The lead must be approximately three to five

feet long and of leather. Be sure not to have too wide a leather lead or the edges will cut your hand as you jerk the dog. The lead must have a strong clip, especially for big dogs. I have had little success with the convenient scissor-type of clip. They are inclined to break when you jerk your dog. Your pet store can recommend the strongest clip.

The next step is to get your dog sitting on your left-hand side. Hold your lead in the right hand, over the two middle fingers only, and adjust the length so that when you are walking with your dog, and you are holding your hand slightly across your body, the lead hangs in a loop. It is vitally necessary to have the lead loose when held in the right hand. Now your left hand is free to do any correcting of the dog that is necessary. Should the dog pull on the lead, let him get nearly to the end of the lead and then put your left hand on the lead with your fingers facing the way you are going and your thumbs facing towards yourself, palm downwards; now with a firm command, 'Heel!' give your dog a very quick jerk back to your side. Take your left hand off the lead immediately; he will be almost certain to forge ahead again, so repeat the quick jerk with the short sharp command 'Heel!' prefaced by the dog's name. Always preface any command with the dog's name, to attract its attention. Also try to keep the dog's attention on its work and position by cheerful encouraging word, such as 'Good boy, close'. Most owners do not jerk their dogs quickly enough, but give a few slow gentle pulls; this is useless, and will never train a dog. Slap your leg to attract the dog's attention, praise it when it comes near to your side, always try the encouraging word before the jerk. Stopping a really bad puller can only be achieved by the most peremptory kind of jerk. It may look rough, but it does not in any way hurt the dog. Most people forget to take their left hands off the lead immediately after the jerk, and therefore spoil the chance of the dog's lead being completely loose after he has been corrected. Always continue walking at a normal pace while jerking. *Never stop to jerk the dog*, or the lesson is spoilt. If the dog drags behind, jerk him forward in the same manner. If a dog lies on the ground when asked to walk, and no amount of encouraging words will make him stand up and come on, go on walking relentlessly, paying no attention to the dog. In no time he will get up and give up being dragged, and you will have defeated him in the first battle of wills.

I know it is easier to write about these things than to carry them out, but I am not keeping back any of the secrets of dog training just because some people think the procedure heartless. If you wish to take your dog out in the street on a loose lead you may have to achieve what you wish by a clash of wills. I recently dealt with a tiny three-pound Griffon whose owner had had to carry her in her arms for six months as she did this lying-down trick. I took her to a carpeted landing and dragged her; in a few seconds, she thought she might do well to mend her ways, and then I took her out for a walk. She has given no trouble ever since. I do not like these battles any more than the owners do, but I feel it my duty to help both owner and dog to live a happier life, and often one short, sharp engagement will do the trick.

There is never, in my opinion, any possible excuse for smacking a dog for bad heel work. If you continue to jerk in the right manner you must win. The time it takes depends on the sharpness of your jerks and your skill as a handler. Having got your dog walking better on the lead, you must now teach him to sit every time you stop. This obviates any chance of the dog causing you to be pulled into the road should you suddenly stop on seeing a vehicle coming, for as you stop, however suddenly, your dog sits. Eventually your dog becomes so well trained that he doesn't need the command 'Sit' as you stop; he knows what to do. But this high degree of training will not be brought about in a week by the average dog owner without experience.

To get your dog to sit quickly and easily, your lead should be of just the right length, so that as you intend stopping you should place your lead, which is held in the right hand, up and over your right hip. This anchors the dog's head in an upward position and helps you to push him to the 'sit' with the free left hand. This movement is done in 'one-two' time. Up with the right hand on the *one,* and down with the left hand on the *two.* Now the correct position of the left hand should be thus: your four fingers are facing away from your leg, and should be placed over the dog's back, so that the two middle fingers are in his flank just in front of the hind leg. The thumb should now be facing towards your own left leg and should also be placed lightly over the dog's back. On your command 'sit', you should, of course, raise your right hand over your right hip and smartly pull the dog down to the 'sit' with the left hand. If you are doing it correctly, the dog cannot do anything but sit. If you are too slow with the left-handed pull, your dog will have got ahead of you and will then be sitting in front of you; this is bad, because you would trip over him as you began to walk again. The secret of a tidy 'sit' beside you is speed; as you stop quickly, pull firmly with the left hand and the right hand goes to your hip. There are, of course, different methods of achieving this 'sit', but I have tried many others and have found the one described infallible for all types of dog and owner. It is just as easily performed by a child as an adult, as the dog is off its balance through having its head raised; and if the actions are done fast enough, it goes to the 'sit' almost before it realizes what it is doing. To get a dog to sit well in to your leg, do your practising with a wall on your left side, and walk fairly close to it. This can be done in the street.

We have got our dog to stop pulling or dragging by jerking the lead; we have got him to sit quickly by pushing him down. This is so far, so good, as long as your dog is on the lead, but how do we progress to getting the same results with the dog off the lead? That can only be done when the dog really walks well on lead, and by that I mean that the dog should have left the jerking stage well behind; on the command 'Heel', you can count on his being close to your side, and when you about turn or left turn, or right turn, your dog should come with you. The next step is to remove the lead and place your dog on a very light long piece of string, so fine that he will not feel that he has any restraint at all. At first he will try to run away; call him in and if he doesn't come scold him sharply and repeat the command 'Heel'. He will soon realize that there's no knowing whether he is on the lead or not. And rather than risk a scolding, he will stay to heel.

In all the above exercises, and after every exercise, please remember to give unlimited praise to your dog. I always tell my pupils to bring the right hand down and scratch the dog's chest after every exercise. Dogs love this, and stay still with a benign expression on their faces as long as you like to continue it.

The next step is to have no lead or string at all on your dog, and to walk about, calling him to stay to heel. If he does so, praise him at once. It is imperative that you never weary your dog of this heel work. Never practise it for more than ten minutes at home. In the street, do not allow your dog to pull you about; if he attempts it, correct him firmly. You are quite certain to have a few busybodies accost you and tell you how cruel you are, but their views are of no importance. I expect they think it kinder that the dog should be free to run across the road and kill himself or someone else. We who really love dogs have to put up with a certain amount of ridicule and criticism from stupid so-called dog lovers who cannot bear even to see a dog corrected. Be comforted, for there are thousands of dogs who hardly need training, they are naturally obedient and well behaved. Their owners are lucky. I, and others like me, are here to deal with the not-so-fortunate owners of adorable but definitely badly behaved dogs.

Do not at any time imagine that the training of a dog to absolute perfection is a matter of a weekend's work. It all depends on your dog's temperament, and your ability to absorb and carry out the instruction given to you.

6: Call Your Dog

The next most important task we have to tackle is to get your dog to come when you call him. This lesson is at first taught on a lead. Put your dog on his lead and tell him to stay; walk back to the full extent of his lead, and then call him up to sit in front of you. If he is unwilling to come a short quick jerk on the lead will pull him to his feet. Encourage him to come to you by putting all the love you can muster into your voice, coupled with a series of quick jerks and the word 'Come' prefaced by his name. If he tries to bolt, jerk him sharply with the word 'Come', changing to a warm, encouraging voice should he show any sign of coming to you. If you think it will help to give him a titbit on coming by all means give him one, but drop this habit as soon as is possible or the dog may get disgruntled later on with coming and not getting anything. This recall exercise must be treated as another lesson, not as a meal!

You have now got your dog to come to you on the lead. 'Sit' him in front so that his head touches your knees, or, according to his size, that part of your leg or body he can reach. My Great Dane touches my chest. Then with your lead still in your right hand, give the dog a cheerful command, 'Heel!' and help him to go round behind you and sit once more on your left-hand side, ready as usual to set off (Plate 9). To get your dog to go round to this position the lead must be passed from the right hand, round the back of you to the left hand, and then back to the right hand so that you can as before push the dog down to the 'sit' with the left hand. If the dog is slow going round behind, you can help him to get there by gently pushing his rump. That means he is being pulled in the right direction with one hand and pushed as an aid with the other hand. I strongly recommend a titbit at first to supplement the reward of your enthusiastic praise when the dog gets to your left side. That left side of you must be the place that the dog comes to associate with love, praise, and the occasional little snack. To get a dog to do this going-to-heel easily, try doing it on a loose lead and flicking the fingers of your right hand as an encouragement, also patting the left thigh to induce him to come there. The less you pull tightly on the lead, the more easily your dog will learn this act.

47

Now you are ready to put the dog on a ten-yard cord and make him come in to you in exactly the same way but from a greater distance. Most dogs find it difficult to stay while their owners leave them to get to the end of the cord. Should the dog get up, go back to him and firmly push him to the 'sit' again. Walk backwards facing him all the time, keeping your finger raised and gently repeating the command, accompanied by his name: 'Stay, Fido' or 'Fido, stay', whichever you like best. When you have at last got him to stay, get to the end of your cord and call him; should he run away, pull him in quickly on your cord and scold him (Plate 10). Then loose him again; at this stage I think he will hesitate, and this is the time to coax and praise him for all you are worth. He thinks this is just the life for him, and usually comes in. Give him a titbit if you want to. If he hesitates and tries to decamp, use his name firmly in a lowered voice, which means (to him) murder if he doesn't obey. At the slightest attempt to come to you, change at once to the loving tone.

I cannot stress too strongly that the tone of your voice is the secret to efficient training. Some people literally cannot alter their voices enough to make their dogs listen to them and perceive a change of mood. Such folk can register neither love nor displeasure. This is a great disadvantage in dog training and makes the handler's task a difficult one. I often say I would like my pupils to leave their dogs at home and come for a voice training lesson before attempting to teach their dogs. People have often asked why their dogs behave well with me and not with them, and I have explained that my tone range makes me sound exciting to the dog, or cross, or adoring, and in each case the dog responds accordingly. I have often demonstrated this by using the most hateful words to a dog in a loving voice, and the tail has wagged in the happiest manner. Alternatively I have said the most loving things in a stern voice, and the dog has cringed and been miserable. In dog training it is *how* you say things, not what you say, that matters.

Your final object is to make the dog come instantly, on command; not, as I have said elsewhere, when he feels he might as well come since there is no more attractive prospect; not simply because he is tired of what he is doing.

We now assume you have got your dog to come on the cord at all times. Next you must get him in an enclosed space and practise with the same tone of voice and commands with him off the lead. A landing is a good place for practice, or an enclosed yard. If he does it well, always take him for a walk in an open space. practise on the cord first of all, and then without the cord. If the dog runs away go back to the cord and practise further. In a subsequent chapter on the question of 'leaving other dogs alone', I shall mention means by which you may make your dog come to you without fuss.

This business of making a dog come when it is called has two aspects. If the dog imagines he is going to get scolded when he does come, he naturally sees no point in coming. So many people, having chased their dogs for ages, at last capture the animals and proceed to beat them. That is fatal. If the dog comes to you, even after an hour, by himself, he must be praised, however evil you feel. If, however, you actually catch the dog as he is bolting away, then you must reprimand him. Most dogs adore being chased and, seeing a pursuer, run all the faster. A great many fall into the trap of hastily following you if, instead of chasing them, you turn round and run in the opposite direction. The dog races after you and a sudden turn round on your part makes a capture possible. I feel very strongly that any dog that runs away from its owner is not attached by that loving bond that should exist between owner and dog. I feel that this dog is one that has been turned or let out in the garden to amuse itself. This sort of treatment is not kindness, but is pure laziness on the part of the owner. The dog's place at all times should be with its owner; left to its own devices it gets into mischief and develops an independent set of habits through being forced to be by itself. I cannot believe that any dog that has the advantage of constantly being with its owner would enjoy running off. It has become used to being a constant friend and companion. We know many people who keep dogs say they are too busy to exercise them, and just turn them out, but I have proved that dogs need very little exercise. It is exercise even if they are merely following some member of the household from room to room as she goes about the usual household tasks.

Many dog owners see their dogs for only a short period each day. They are too busy to do otherwise. Are we, in spite of such a drawback, to deny these people the companionship of a dog when they come home in the evening? I think not, but I do think they cannot, on such terms, expect the dog to obey them instantly when so little of their lives is shared with the dog. It is particularly these people who should spend time in the evenings practising the art of training and getting to know their dogs better. Some dogs have the natural hunting instinct deeply ingrained and it is these dogs that are the most dangerous to domestic livestock, and the least to be relied upon, without training, to return to the owner on command. Such dogs should be given a great deal of work of some kind to divert these natural instincts. A dog that does advanced obedience training, and receives much deserved praise, gets this joy and energy expenditure in such work, but other dogs just get into mischief. The trouble is that owners buy the wrong sort of dog for their circumstances. Often you see someone with a greyhound, for example, a dog which everyone knows is not a quiet household pet but a breed with a job of work to do, and best kept for their work as a foxhound is for his, whereas the owner, who wants a quiet steady house dog, should try another more placid type. I have not picked on greyhounds for any particular reason except that thay are so beautiful that many buyers cannot resist them, so that they are bought without any idea of their inheritance and requirements.

I expect a good many owners will be annoyed or distressed to read that I believe their dogs do not really love them enough if they prefer freedom to the owner's company; but they might reflect that bars and clubs are filled on most evenings with somewhat similar human beings, who prefer the company of acquaintances to that of their wives. Dogs can be 'almost human'!

7 : 'Sit' and 'Down' Exercises :
Training Your Dog to 'Wait'

By now, having got your dog to walk to heel on and off the lead, you can progress to one of the most difficult of exercises, that of teaching your dog to stay at the 'sit' or the 'down' when you go out of sight. This is essential with a town dog who likes to accompany his mistress shopping. Many shops nowadays, regardless of licked fingers and of hands unwashed after noseblowing, and so forth, not to mention ash-dropping customers, pin up notices requesting that 'in the interests of health, will customers not bring their dogs into the shop'. So far as untrained dogs are concerned, I agree wholeheartedly. Some dog owners are indescribably lax in allowing their dogs to lift their legs and soil over shop doors, and even over vegetables in shops. It is thanks to this sort of owner that decent, right-minded owners must also keep their dogs outside. As this exclusion is now general in many districts we should all endeavour to train our dogs so that they can accompany us so far, and yet comply with the shopkeeper's request. It is quite easy to train your dog to sit or lie down outside a shop; harder to train is the general public who cannot leave your dog in peace. It takes years of training to get a dog to that state of training where it will stay put under the most trying circumstances. In my classes I attempt to emulate the public, I bend down and stroke the dogs, I drop my handbag near them, I climb over them, I walk other dogs all round them, and generally do my best to upset them. But the trouble is that as they know me, the test is not strict enough. If it were possible to practise with strangers, the lesson would have more value.

Here is the way to begin training your dog to wait outside for you. If you had him as a puppy, you would already, we hope, have carried out the instructions for making him stay alone in another room, but I am going to presume you have only just acquired an adult dog, and are about to train him to wait. Get out the familiar cord so useful in dog training. Put your dog again on to it, and as he has already learnt to 'stay' while you go the end of the cord (in the recall) repeat this as the beginning of the exercise. Then return to him while he is still on the cord and immediately leave him again, at first giving him the command 'Stay!' as you leave. Should he get up, push him down again, and leave him again. Get him thoroughly used to this, and then if you have a garden put him to 'sit' or 'down' in the garden and walk into the house. Watch him, and the moment he moves, shout 'down' from your window without letting him see you. He will not know where the voice is coming from, but will probably drop again, comforted by the fact that you are about. Every time he moves repeat the command, then return to him, keeping him 'down' until you are right up to him, and then let him up and praise him for all you are worth.

Never leave a dog at the 'sit' for more than two minutes: it is a tiring performance. If you intend leaving the dog for longer than that, put him to the 'down'. This is easier to write than to accomplish. I am always surprised at the number of dogs who strenuously resist being made to lie down. Why, I can't imagine, for it is a natural and restful position. There are several ways, no doubt, of putting a dog 'down'. I use two. The first is a simple if rather slow method, and a good one to start on. The second is a quicker but more difficult method, mostly used by those having to deal with very strong dogs. I use the command 'down', for I detest the word 'flat': it is a hard, uncomfortable word. 'Down' can be a caress and an assurance all in one, and if ever a dog needs assurance it is when a loved owner leaves him alone. I have seen owners in murderous temper with their dogs in the show ring obedience tests when the dog has got up when supposed to be lying down, but I believe that this happens because the dog has not trusted its owner enough. It is frightened lest maybe the owner should not come back. Do not we human beings feel worried enough to go a hundred times to the door when a loved one is late coming home? Such anxiety is quite understandable. Yet a dog must not have any such fears, and if he dares to get up and look around him, he is punished. I know he must learn this exercise for his safety's sake, but I wish owners would give more comforting words to their dogs as they leave them. I see owners leaving their dogs without a smile or a backward glance, and uttering the most aloof 'Stay', yet they expect the dog to be happy while awaiting their return. Leave your dog with a pat and a kind word, give it a very slow firm command, 'Stay'. Don't leave it and go out of sight until it will stay for a long time with you still in sight; then slowly go farther and farther away. Should the dog get up when you are still in sight, then is the time to be firm and rather cross. He has no excuse for anxiety when he can see you, and is showing disobedience that must be firmly checked. No soft 'Do lie down for Mummy's sake' is any good in this case; a firm command and push down are indicated.

To get a dog to lie down without frightening or hurting himself or you in any way, put him at the 'sit', then lift one foreleg with one hand and gently push the opposite shoulder towards the leg you are raising. (Plate 11). This puts the dog off its balance and it has to go down. As soon as it is down scratch its chest, and praise it. The second way to make a dog lie down if it is walking on your left side is to grasp the running end of the choke chain in the right hand still holding the lead, turn the hand until the palm faces ahead of the dog's nose, stand facing your dog's side with legs wide apart for balance; in this position, place your hand on the ground a few inches ahead of the dog and with the other hand press on its back; the pressure on the choke chain forces the dog's head down and the back pressure helps to overbalance it. Usually it only takes a minute or two to teach a dog this, if you use a firm command 'down' at the same time exerting the pressure on collar and back. I definitely prefer the first shoulder-pushing method for beginners, but the other method is quick and easy if you do it with lightning speed, and of course it does get your dog lying down directly beside you in a crouching position, whereas the shoulder-pushing method gets the dog down in a 'curled over' position. This latter position, incidentally, is quite essential if you intend leaving a dog for a long time. A crouching dog can get up quickly, but a dog in the 'curled' position has first to get into the crouching position before it can rise. If you use the lead method of dropping your dog, gradually get the lead longer and less tight. I find that after I have done this about six times, a dog will drop on my placing my hand on the ground in front of it, anticipating the tug on its collar which it finds unpleasant. The third method is to stand beside your dog raising the right hand holding the lead, and placing the left foot over the running end of the choke chain quickly pulling the dog to the ground (Plate 12).

In teaching your dog to stay outside shops it is essential to get the help of friends who will accustom the dog to having strangers walk near it, and perhaps bend down and touch it. That is one of the great advantages of a training class. So many people are rushing back to their dogs, or yelling at them, or falling over them, that the dogs get used to the most fantastic noise and disturbances. I have noticed in classes that no one thinks of the possibility of anyone else's dog getting upset by his sudden rush to reprimand his own dog. This, of course, certainly helps to train the other handlers' dogs, for there is no chance here for a nervous dog to show temperament. The extraordinary thing is that I have constantly found the most nervous dogs forgetting their nerves in this mêlée and becoming quite used to strangers jumping over them. Biting dogs no longer bite passers by; in fact, the relentless bustle and constant motion and uproar seem to help a nervous dog, rather than make it worse.

As I have said before, a good deal of patience will be required before you will be able safely to leave your dog outside a shop. You need to practise it by leaving it with its lead still attached at first, and keeping a watchful eye on it all the time. But with practice it will learn to ignore all passers-by.

In this book I have often used the words 'scold' or 'get cross with' your dog; this may mean just switching to a sad tone of voice while using his name, or even putting on a shocked look, or addressing him with a flood of cross words, or giving him a shaking. It all depends on the nature of the bond between you and your dog. If you are an owner who only talks to his dog when the rare mood takes you, you will probably have to use far harsher methods than someone who has a dog that is spoken to at every hour of the day and really understands change of tone and even expression. If I say 'Junia' in a sad voice and don't smile when I say it, my dog is sufficiently punished and slinks off in shame; but then she really understands my words and moods; we share our lives completely; she worries with me, she rejoices with me, and if she does wrong, she knows without my scolding that I am annoyed. Only a forgiving word will make her happy again, and I never prolong my disapproval for more than a minute or two, as she would be sick with sorrow if I did.

8 : Dog Fights and Ignoring Other Dogs

Now we have arrived at one of the most difficult tasks of all in dog training. It is natural that dogs should wish to sniff each other as they pass. But if we are to have a dog that is safe on and off the lead and which can be safely left in the street, we must teach him to pay no attention to other dogs unless we give him the command 'Play', when he is at liberty to romp until called away with the command 'Leave'.

It is much easier to teach a dog to ignore others in a training class, as we divide the class into two sections, one at each end of the room; and on the command 'Forward' they walk forward and pass through the line of dogs opposite them, so that the dogs pass beside one another. We call this exercise 'countermarching'. As the dogs approach each other if one even looks at the other, a firm command 'Leave' is given, and a sharp jerk on the offender's choke chain. If this exercise is repeated again and again, and the dog always receives a jerk just before it sniffs the other dog, he is left with the impression that it is rather unpleasant to talk to another dog in such circumstances.

I have cured fighters by this method in a very short time. But the real difficulty lies in knowing when your dog is going to fight; it is useless to take such steps once the dogs have come to grips with each other. How many people are sufficiently knowing with their dogs to sense the stiffening of the body which is preliminary to a fight? Too many owners usually wait until the fight has started before doing anything about it. That is why it is a good thing for an experienced trainer to have the first chance, especially in a class, to check this fighting tendency. But wherever they are, if owners really know their dogs they will sense the stiffening of the dog as he approaches another, the dog's way of sending out a warning to the other one that he is ready to hold his own against all comers. A dog that has no intention of fighting is relaxed. One that is not sure but wishes to be friendly keeps up a very fast but confined wagging of its tail as it approaches another dog; this will stop, and the dog will stiffen, if the enemy has evil ideas, and is not reciproacting the offer of friendship. Most dogs approach a bitch in this way, hoping for friendship, and although it is unusual for a dog and bitch to fight, the bitch may attack first and then the dog will answer back, but usually not for very long. A growl, of course, must never be ignored. A fight inevitably follows unless checked, but an owner must be able to read far less obvious indications than the growl and the snarl if he is to stop fights at the right moment—that is, before they have begun.

This business of making your dog ignore others needs constant vigilance; a second's carelessness, and you are in a fight. I believe that if a dog does get involved in a fight he should be severely punished unless he was obviously attacked first. Therefore, as I hate to advocate punishing dogs, it is the owner's duty to see that no fight develops. It is a fatal move to tighten your lead as another dog approaches, and even worse to lift your dog up. Walk on quite naturally until reasonably near the other dog, then give a sharp jerk on your dog's collar to arrest his attention, and in a firm, low voice, command 'Leave'. There is nothing more I can tell you about how to prevent a fight. It is up to the owner to be wary. But I can advise you on how to separate dogs if they are in a fight. The best method I know is to seize hold of the dog's skin on the forehead, an extremely painful hold on a tender spot, and the dog will instantly release the other dog, when you can drag it away. Hitting makes matters worse. Pepper, the old cure, one doesn't carry about with one, and a bucket of water is hardly ever to be found in the middle of the street or in a park. Another cure, people tell me, is to choke your dog. I wouldn't be brave enough to try it, chiefly on account of the risk of being bitten by the other dog. I have separated many fighting dogs in my time, and I always use the method I recommend.

Quite a number of people want to know whether they can really cure a confirmed fighter so that it may safely be allowed to run freely with other dogs. I should say no. A dog can be so far cured as to be safe at all times when under the control of its owner. We have often trained fighters to be safely left in a hall with thirty or more other dogs lying all together, all the owners out of sight, but all the dogs in the room had had training, therefore the fighter was not getting challenges or rude remarks thrown at it by other dogs. However, I would not like to say that the former fighter, if attacked, would not fight to the finish. I think he would, and only a terrific amount of disciplinary training would make it safe at all times. I have cured (to the point of their becoming very nice dogs to take out without a lead) dogs that were previously bad fighters; one had even killed another dog, but it had a sensible owner. It must depend to a great extent on the owner's temperament. If the owner is always nervous, the dog will always be on his guard against aggression; if the owner is confident that her dog is cured of its vice, the dog will gain assurance from that attitude, and be far less likely to want to fight. I think fighting, with biting of owners, postmen and visitors, are all attributable together to the one complaint; nerves and insecurity. The dog has probably not been taken out and about enough in its youth; to make a dog reliable, it should be taken into towns and crowds, shops and parks, and wherever you live, it must be allowed to meet other dogs. Let people caress it and talk to it. Be firm if it slinks away and won't talk to people; show it that human beings are its friends; if possible find a friendly neighbour's dog and let it have romps with it, making sure that on command it leaves off playing and comes back to you. Such a dog will never be a fighter: why should it be? Big dogs are often put on a very short lead and held in a vicelike grip in the street. Times without number I have shown owners that a fighter on a loose lead seldom attacks, but they are so scared that they daren't let up on the stranglehold. Naturally, if you get a big dog involved in a fight, it takes plenty of courage and strength to end the battle. I once separated two dogs, and then one got hold of my leg, thinking it was the other dog, and I couldn't let go of the second or the fight would have started all over again. Luckily someone took one dog from me while I prised the other off my leg, but I still bear the scar.

I think fighting is, to a certain extent, an inherited temperamental fault, and I strongly advise buyers of dogs to enquire about the parents' temperaments before buying a puppy. Fighters are always of a bullying nature, and therefore need from an early age a strict code of discipline. Any sign of rolling on their backs, and biting the owner or its lead when the lead has to go on, is often the prelude to serious biting or fighting later in life. I am always dead against allowing a dog to use its teeth on me even in play, and any attempt to answer back with its teeth when I give a command is instantly checked.

I often feel that dogs bite and fight to let off steam. Many live such restricted lives that they become psychological cases weighed down by repressions. In such circumstances, human beings lose their tempers or burst into tears, but dogs are allowed no such outlet. I feel that a dog that leads a fully occupied life as a complete member of the owner's family never gets these vices, having plenty of legitimate interests to keep it stable.

If a dog continues to fight at the slightest pretext after an owner has followed all my recommendations, I should say he was incurable, and the owner must decide whether to keep him, and always be on guard against a fight, and the risk of his causing harm which may end up in the law courts, or whether to have him put to sleep to end its unhappy existence. I hate to advocate putting a dog down at any time, and only the owner can decide on a matter of this kind.

Most fighters are what they are through bad handling by inexperienced owners. Once the habit is firmly established it takes an experienced handler to cure it, but a fighting dog is an unsafe dog at all times, even a partially 'cured' one.

9 : 'Waiting on Command'

This exercise is really an advanced one used in Test C in competition work, when it is called 'Advance Stand, Sit, and Down'. Here we are going to study it in relation to its usefulness to the ordinary dog owner. The idea is to make your dog stop instantly on command when you are in motion, either at the 'stand', 'sit' or 'down', so that you can run or walk on without it, and without worrying about its behaviour. There may come an emergency in your life when this exercise might save someone's life. You might, for example, see a small child toddle into the street in the path of a car; with the command 'Wait' your dog would instantly stand still, and un-hampered you could rescue the child from its peril. On the other hand, you might just want to leave your dog in the drive for a second and run back to get something from the house without his coming; on the command 'Wait' he would stay where he was until your return.

We teach this exercise in class by having helpers who walk behind the handler and dog, and on the trainer's command 'Now' the handler drops the lead near the helper, who places a foot on it, and with a firm command 'Wait', the dog is left in the standing position until the handler has made a circle and returned to the dog. He picks up the lead, and with the command 'Heel' and a word of praise continues walking. On the next command, 'Now' from the trainer, the handler repeats the exercise with the dog this time put quickly to the 'Sit'. And so it is repeated, at the third time the dog being put to the 'down' (Plate 13). The idea is to teach your dog to stop instantly and to expect the owner back in a reasonably short time. It is quite amazing how quickly dogs learn this exercise. I find the 'stand' is the most difficult to teach them as they have learnt before this to sit at all times when not walking. If your dog sits when you wish him to stand, run your left hand quickly under his tummy and lift him to the 'stand' with a further command, 'Wait!'. He won't mind this, and it soon teaches him. Don't forget to give the command 'Wait' in a quick tone not a long drawn-out voice. Emphasize the 't' in the word 'Sit' and the 'D' in the command 'Down'.

When your dog has got used to being left with the helper, who must in no way touch your dog (he is only acting as an anchor), the next step is to leave your dog without a helper, but with the lead on. You must practise alone in a room or your garden until the dog never moves until you come back. Next of course, you must take the lead off and repeat the exercise again. Practise it at a walking pace and then at a run. At the end of the three exercises give your dog a vast amount of praise. I use cheerful words in the middle of the exercise, like 'good boy' (or 'girl') so that the dog will realize he has not finished after one part of the exercise. But at the end of the three commands well carried out I bubble over with joy and praise!

I think that to teach this exercise correctly you must know how to teach your dog to stand, sit or lie down, at a distance. This exercise is most important to all dog owners, as sooner or later a time comes in all our lives when a loved dog races out to greet master or mistress on their return home, and this exuberance may be the death of the dog or of someone on the road, if the dog is so excited that it forgets to look before dashing across the road. But if the dog has been trained to drop into the sit or down position on a hand signal or by voice, you have a reasonable chance of stopping its rush to you when danger threatens.

This exercise (with Obedience Test fans) is called 'Distant Control', and I shall enlarge on it in the next few pages.

10 : Distant Control

I teach the handlers in my class to do this exercise in a long line, with their dogs at the end of the lead facing them. But it can be done alone at home just as easily. I give the command 'Now' and the handlers give their dogs the same command as my next. Should I say 'Down', the handlers must raise their right hands and bring them sharply to the ground with the command 'down'; the dogs must instantly drop to this position. They should do this without fuss if they have been trained step by step from this book. My next command may be 'Sit': the owners must repeat it to their dogs, and in doing so give the command by voice and the signal by raising their right hands from the ground to above the head (Plate 14). The command 'Sit' should be given in a short quick word, not drawn-out like the command 'Down'. Change of tone of voice (I cannot say this too often) matters enormously in these exercises. If the dog does not go quickly to the 'sit', help him up by lifting him on the lead which should have been under his chin anyway, or by touching his front foot nails lightly with your foot so that he naturally breaks away into the 'sit'.

Next I shall give the command 'Stand'. The owner repeats the command and the signal is a slap on the thigh of one leg, which encourages the dog to begin to come to you (Plate 15). As soon as the dog is standing, check him coming (Plate 15) towards you with the command 'Stay', which of course he should now know. Should the dog not stand, run your hand between his front legs along his chest to his tummy, and lift him up on to his back legs. Alternatively, lift him up with both hands placed just inside his back legs at the thigh and stand him firmly on his legs. As your dog improves on the lead, put him on the cord and do the whole thing at a greater distance. He will at first try to advance towards you; this must be checked with the command 'Stay', after the ordinary command. Even in competition work the dog is allowed six feet to move forward so don't worry too much at first if he can't stick to this; it is a goal to work for. If he came too far forward in the street he would get run over. I should teach a small dog on a table, a large one at the top of the stairs, so that they can't come forward. Eventually, when

61

the dog does the exercise well, remove the cord and do it again with the dog free. We do six successive commands. Never repeat this exercise *ad nauseam*, for it is very tiring for the dog and requires great concentration on the part of the owner and dog. Once the dog has learnt it well, abandon it except for an occasional reminder. I hope you will never need to make much use of it.

Having accomplished the teaching of distant control, you want to practise it by leaving your dog at a distance, calling him, and when he's running quickly towards you, giving him the signal and command 'Down'. If you have trained him properly he should drop instantly and wait for you to call him up when all is safe. In Obedience Trials this is called 'Drop on Recall'; it may be done there either by word or signal, but not both. I strongly disagree with this. I fail to see that in an emergency an owner wouldn't use a command and signal if the dog's or somebody's life depended on it, but then I am an outlaw where these fantastic rules are concerned. I love to see a dog working, but I like it only when it is a joint effort of understanding and brains on the part of both dog and owner. These silent masters and mistresses in the obedience ring can keep their dogs that way if they wish, but I defy anyone to say that the dog likes it. I believe that those dogs, bouncing about as if they were happy, are really a mass of nerves wondering whether they have done right. I am not a 'sour grapes'; my former dog won sixty-seven of these Tests, but she and I hated every one of them. It was only that in order to be able to train other people and dogs, one had to prove that one could train one's own dog first. This is the only reason I took part in these tests. Some people think it is cruel to teach a dog tricks. My dog does endless tricks; and how she loves doing things for me! She arches her neck in pride when she has done something particularly clever, and wants to hear me say so. I love praise if I have done something well; so do children, and so do animals. If I am working her in a film she can't wait until after the Director has said 'Cut' to dash round to everyone in the studio to hear how clever she has been. I can teach my dog anything new in a few minutes, and providing I can talk to her and praise her immediately after doing it, she adores it.

Opinion is divided about teaching dogs tricks. Is it cruel, people ask? I fail to see that cruelty comes into it unless the tricks taught are for a circus or some such affair when the dog has to perform at a fixed time however little he may feel like doing so. Most dogs love the household tricks we all know, asking for food by begging or barking, playing hide and seek, trusting, etc. I think they join in the family spirit which encourages this harmless fun. A dog already trained in simple obedience is so very easily taught tricks, and I think likes 'being clever'. If he does not enjoy them, then I think it is cruel to force him to become a performer.

11 : Training Your Dog to 'Retrieve' and 'Seek Back'

This is another exercise which I think most dog owners should teach their dogs. Its practical advantage is that if you happen to be out walking and drop something, your dog will go back and look for it and retrieve it. Most of the dogs who come to my class and are given a dumb-bell for the first time, rush after it and joyfully pick it up. Some even bring it back to their owners. But it is these eager dogs who are the first to get tired of doing it, and who have to start all over again later. So we are going to teach our dogs the right way from the beginning and ignore their natural desire to retrieve, which may soon peter out if not properly directed.

First of all we use a dumb-bell, because it has big ends to make the centre bar stand up off the ground; this enables the dog to pick it up easily. The dog must never be allowed to pick it up by the ends or chew it. I keep my own high up on a shelf, and as I give it to my dog I use an excited tone of voice as if it were the greatest treat to be allowed to retrieve dumb-bells!

Now we begin with the dog on the lead at the 'sit'. Gently open the dog's mouth by inserting your finger into the side of the mouth where there are no teeth, immediately behind the large canine tooth, always keeping your hand on top of the dog's nose, not trying to pull down the bottom jaw. When the mouth is open pop the dumb-bell in with the other hand. *Don't push it back into the Dog's mouth*, just balance it behind the canine teeth and allow the dog to close its mouth on it. If you shove it roughly into the mouth you will frighten and hurt the dog, and your task will become more difficult. Should the dog try to spit it out, as most of them do, put it firmly back with the command 'Hold'; to help him do this, scratch his chest with the other hand, for dogs will hold dumb-bells for a long time so long as this pleasant scratching continues. Their docility enables you to say 'Give' in a kind voice and take the dumb-bell away. Always take it out of the dog's mouth with two hands, holding the ends, never with one hand only. Repeat this, making the dog hold the object until he does so quite happily. I often advocate a titbit after he has held it well. The next step is to make him walk holding the dumb-bell. If you can get him to stay holding it when he is at the end of your long cord, and then make him bring it to you, you have surmounted a real difficulty. But if not, just be satisfied for the time being with getting him to walk beside you holding it, tell him to sit, still holding it, and then taking it away with the 'Give' command. Praise him ardently if he has done it well. Some dogs are unbelievably stubborn over this exercise, and will not hold the dumb-bell. They spit it out and fight to avoid holding it. But dozens of times I have made a dog hold a dumb-bell when the owner has failed, and this is done only by showing the dog that your will is every bit as strong as his, and that if necessary you will go on until midnight if he means to defer holding it that long. In the end I always win, but that is more than I can say for many handlers with weaker wills and less determination than I have. Patience, firmness and love are the essentials.

We will presume you are a good handler and that your dog now holds the dumb-bell as soon as it is given to him. Next, you have to teach him to pick it up. This is done by standing beside your dog, and with one hand holding the dog's scruff, or loose skin on the neck, while gently pushing his head down until his mouth is over the dumb-bell. Then, with the other hand, you open his mouth by inserting the first finger into the side of the mouth, and pop the dumb-bell into his mouth with the second finger. Let him close his mouth and tell him to 'hold'. Eventually your dog opens his own mouth as you push his head down, and later on, with infinite care and encouragement and practice, your dog will pick it up himself. Once he has accomplished this, give the command 'hold' and run backwards; the dog will follow you, holding the dumb-bell. Turn round sharply and tell him to sit; push him down if he doesn't do it quickly enough, still telling him to 'hold'. Then take the dumb-bell with the word 'Give' and send your dog behind you to your usual left-hand side. Now you are getting on. There is one enormous fence still to get over, and that is the sending of your dog to fetch the dumb-bell. The best way I know is for you to get a friend to help. Ask your friend to hold on to the long cord on which you have put your dog; you must then make the dog sit by your side, throw your dumb-bell, and encourage the dog to go after it. If the dog won't do so, get your friend to pull the dog towards the dumb-bell on the cord. The dog should now, receiving much praise, pick up the dumb-bell and return to you, sitting in front holding it quietly until you take it, after which you will send the dog to heel on your left side. It doesn't usually take long for the dog to understand this 'going' part of the exercise. Lastly, you must teach it not to go after the dumb-bell that they must not chase moving things without command. If this precaution is neglected, one day the children may be playing ball with the dog in the garden, and the ball may roll out into the road; and then, if the dog is untrained, it would rush after it. A trained dog waits for the command to get it. I usually recommend owners to hold their dogs by their collars and give the command 'Wait' until the dog understands what is wanted of him, and will sit quietly after the dumb-bell has been thrown until given the command 'Fetch'.

Before we can go any further with the 'seek-back' exercise, which consists of making your dog retrace your steps and find what you have dropped, you must teach it only to pick up your article carrying your scent; otherwise it may bring someone else's property, not yours. This exercise is called 'scent discrimination' in official circles, so I shall use this name.

12 : Scent Discrimination or Finding Owner's Dropped Article

Most dogs enjoy this. The best way to teach a dog this exercise is once more to enlist other people to put articles on the floor, or on the grass. Use such things as purses, clothes pegs, match boxes, gloves, handkerchiefs, in fact anything the dog might come in contact with in everyday life. Next you decide what you wish the dog to find, let's say your glove. Place the glove, for a minute or two prior to doing the exercise, under your armpit, it will then pick up a good scent of you. Next, without letting the dog see it, place it among the other articles, not too closely jumbled at first. Then take the dog on its lead up to the articles, pointing to each one as you walk by it, saying, with some excitement, 'Seek', 'Good boy, seek'. Use a most inspiriting tone, as though rats were his quarry. Usually when the dog reaches its owner's article he grabs it, and then you should praise him immediately; but should he pass it by, return to it, and show it to him, pick it up and use it to play with him. Then take him away, get it put down for you again, and try once more. This time he is almost certain to find the right article, so praise him and have a game with it. Continue like this, with different articles all the time, until he knows that he must only find the one carrying your scent. Should he attempt to pick up the wrong article, say 'No' crossly, take it away, and show him the right one. As soon as your dog has learnt thus to pick out your particular article only, teach him to bring it back to you as with the dumb-bell; and, as before, 'sit' in front and go round to heel to finish with. Now that we have taught the dog to find and retrieve any article, we are ready to teach him the 'seek back'. Go for a walk, and on your way drop something on the path that shows up well—for instance, a handkerchief. Walk on about twenty yards and in a very excited tone of voice tell the dog to 'seek back', pointing to where you have come from. The dog probably won't understand, so run back, encouraging him to go away and seek all the time. Nine times out of ten he sees the handkerchief and picks it up. Then you must praise him with extravagant enthusiasm. Make him do this quite often on your walk; he will soon understand and enjoy the game. As he gets better at it, hide the article in grass near where you have been. That will teach him to cast round and look. Make it more difficult as the dog gets to understand, and you will soon have taught your dog something that may be very useful. One of my friends recently lost her house keys in a wood. She had trained her dog, and he went back over her tracks and found them. Needless to say, she was delighted.

There remains only one exercise in the obedience test schedule to be learnt now, and that is the 'send away'. Its uses, in my opinion, are few. Perhaps it teaches your dog to go straight home should he insist on following you when you leave home and want him to stay behind. In Test C at shows the dog must go on a single command or signal in a dead straight line and continue going until you are told to drop him down. He must drop to the ground and stay there with you walking past him until you call him up. Marks are lost for a deviation from a straight line, no extra commands are allowed to change the dog's direction should he be going crooked, or you lose marks. This seems to me a pointless exercise. But as some of my readers enjoy competitions, I shall do my best to teach the necessary handling for this lesson.

13 : 'Send Away' : A Brief Note on a Lengthy Routine

I teach this on the long cord again if the dog shows no signs of leaving you when you say 'Away' or 'Go'. Our dog has already learnt to go and fetch the dumb-bell, leaving you in order to do so, so it shouldn't be too difficult to go a step further and make them go and 'fetch' nothing. Let us assume that the dog will not budge at all. The trainer or helper must take the cord, as usual, some distance away from the dog. The dog is sitting quietly on the left-hand side of the owner and is given the command 'Away' with the right arm pointing in the direction he is supposed to go; if he does not move, help him by repeating the command and giving him a simultaneous shove in the right direction. Keep repeating 'Away', and stamp your foot as if you were going to chase him. He doesn't understand. Very well, ask your friend to pull him on in the cord, while you keep pointing and saying 'Away'. When he has gone a little distance, give him the command 'Down'. He should know this, and drop; walk up to him, telling him to stay, walk round him and away, and then call him to heel. Praise him.

Sometimes one can shortcut this method by another one. This is to put your dog at the 'sit', tell him to stay, and walk away some distance where he can see what you are doing, bend down and rub your hand vigorously on the ground, come back to your dog, and give him the 'Away' command. Very often he will rush off to see what you did; you can then drop him and the exercise is begun. I find the other method better. This 'Away' exercise takes a long time to teach and reach perfection.

14 : Difficult Dogs

INTRODUCTORY NOTE

In all my books, broadcasts and television appearances I seem to be forever slanging the owners of disobedient dogs for allowing their dogs to get the better of them. Here I want to lay a bouquet at the feet of all the hundreds of these dog-lovers who, whilst admitting they are probably to blame, do everything within their power to make the life of their dogs happy. They forsake their families to come often hundreds of miles with their dogs to attend a training course, they read, mark, learn and inwardly digest the instruction given to them. If the knowledge given sometimes causes indigestion of the facts at least they have tried. Personally it has given me enormous pleasure to meet these friendly and lovable people. In our mutual desire to make their dogs good we have found a lasting friendship. If some of them haven't always approved of my methods, or I of their handling, we have parted. I well remember one lady who walked out in the middle of a course when I have made a rather sarcastic reference to her ability as a trainer. I naturally thought that was the last I should see of her. Some ten years later she turned up on a course saying her former dog was so good could she bring her new puppy? Needless to say I was delighted at the return of the lost sheep, and from that moment her handling was excellent. Which all goes to show you must be able to take criticism if you wish to progress fast. I know most training clubs don't bully their members like I do, but if one is to handle the maximum numbers in a year one cannot be slow in training owners and dogs. To those who have given me enormous satisfaction and pleasure by letting me handle them and their dogs I say 'thank you'. To those who still need help I say, if you are willing to learn by others' mistakes, and you really want a good dog, I can assure you your dog is possible to train. I hope *Dog Training My Way* with this supplement will guide you and your dog to a mutual and happy partnership.

To be a good trainer or handler of dogs you have to have overwhelming love for them, you have to have the patience of Job, but also that little spark of strong will that doesn't take defeat too easily. If you don't possess these qualifications, don't fret too much, you can soon develop them; if not, with reasonable luck your dog can be trained to train you.

WHY BAD DOGS?

When I had finished the manuscript of the first part of this book, I sent it to my mother. Her remark after reading it was that although she had enjoyed it as a book, she felt certain no one would need it, as surely everyone knew how to train their dogs. Time has shown that not only do people not know how to train their dogs, but that in increasing numbers they own 'problem dogs' and are in need of specialized help and advice. That is why I wrote this addition. In it I shall tackle the difficulties that are met with by people who own problem dogs, and need a little more knowledge to deal with them.

In the hundreds of letters I receive the phrase 'difficult dog' occurs time and time again, hence the title of this chapter. Many of the writers tell me that they have owned dogs for thirty years or more and have never come up against such stubborn, 'wilful, vicious', or such-like dogs before. They all, without exception, imagine that their dog stands out on its own as a unique example of canine wickedness. If only they could read my daily post they would know their letters are repeated almost word for word by many hundreds of dog owners all over the world. What they are unwilling to believe at first is that their dog is no worse than dozens of others, and that if it is 'difficult', the reason can often be placed on their own doorstep. I still maintain, and always shall maintain, that with the exception of dogs which have some physical or mental abnormality, there is not one that cannot be made a good companion by the right training— that is IF the owner can be trained. During the last ten years I have trained 13,000 dogs and owners, and my heart bleeds for the so-called problem dogs brought to me for correction. In most cases the dog can be taught all that is necessary in a very few minutes. When *I* work it, using a thrilling happy tone of voice, the dog works happily with tail wagging, and an expectant interested look on its face. When it errs I use the tone of voice that means 'I win or else' and few dogs fail to recognize that voice and that look on my face. But hand this same dog back to its inexperienced owner and the picture changes. Why? Firstly because it is the nature of our people in recent years to put up with more from our children and our dogs. Next, kindness to animals has been drummed into us as a nation for a long time, and many owners mix up in their minds the true meaning of kindness. Is it kinder to allow a dog to make human lives and its own a misery, rather than to correct it firmly on a choke chain for a few minutes, thereby making it understand clearly who is boss?

I wouldn't hesitate to answer this question. I would say, 'Correct the dog quickly and firmly, and then love it with everything you possess, and the dog will worship you in return.' Dither weakly in the mistaken idea that all bad dogs can be trained by endearing words and you might just as well give up the idea of training a BAD DOG. Remember, writing this I am not dealing with the normal puppy or young dog, or with the experienced owner to whom training a dog is as easy as eating his breakfast.

There is no doubt in my mind that, due to the vast increase in the number of dogs being bred today, and the conditions under which these dogs are housed, a type of dog that should never have been bred is being produced by breeders for sale to the public. The professional breeders cannot be excused for doing this. They should know better than to breed from bitches or dogs with bad temperaments, thus passing on trouble. The amateur breeders still believe the old wives' tale that to breed from a nervous or bad-tempered bitch improves its temperament. What they don't know or don't care about is that they are filling countries with unstable, neurotic and unreliable dogs which are causing thousands of dog lovers misery, and keeping me and others like me glued to our typewriters and our training classes, trying to right the wrongs that should never be met with in normal dogs. But in spite of what I say about the breeding of these dogs, I still believe that if the owners knew how to train them these faults could easily and quickly be eradicated.

There is however one thing I cannot teach a dog, and that is to love its owner. I meet many hundreds of dogs in a year who seem to have no affection for their owner whatsoever. These dogs have to be taught to obey their owners more or less by fear—of the results of disobedience. How very sad it is to find such a relationship. It tears my heart strings when the dog's eyes light up when it meets me, and it shrieks with joy when I kneel down to caress and kiss it.

How is it possible to feed and house a dog, and presumably to love it, and get no affection in return? The answer is respect. Without respect there is little love in the animal kingdom. An animal must always have a boss to love and respect. Some breeds of dog need to respect their owners more than others, some are naturally docile and obedient.

I am going to deal with the many types of problem that are presented to me by dog owners in person or by letter. On reading what I say many indignant owners will deny that they come under any of the categories I mention. Many more will insist that their dog is more wicked than any of those that I talk about, and that theirs could not be cured by the means I recommend. Some will write to me and say they have tried everything and are quite sure that their dog would be my Waterloo. I willingly accept such challenges, if the owners are willing to bring their dog to me for five minutes. For in those five minutes I will find out who is to blame for the 'problem dog', and if I think there is no future happiness for dog and owner in that particular partnership, I will admit it quite freely. For make no mistake, there is no future in many of these dog and owner relationships. The reasons are numerous; one of the most common is a fear of the dog, fear of the dog fighting, or biting, or both. Unless the owner can master his own fear there is no hope for the dog.

In this chapter I am going to tackle all these problems in bulk form. They have been chosen by me from many thousands of letters which I have pigeonholed under this or that type of owner or dog. The variations on the problems are numerous, but in spite of what people think, the same training works for all the different vices. Naturally every dog and owner has slightly different troubles which may need slight variations in handling, but the principle does not vary.

DIFFICULT OWNERS

Before going further into the handling of 'difficult dogs' let us for a few moments analyse the owners of these misfits, and see if we can tackle the problem by re-educating the owners. Without a moment's hesitation I say 'Yes we can'. If the owners are interested enough and fond enough of their dogs to read training books or to attend training schools or courses, or even to write to me, they are well worth the time spent in helping them.

For the most part those who seek my help and advice are women. The female of the species undoubtedly not only wields the rolling pin, but holds the dog's lead as well.

Older children I find make excellent handlers of dogs, but owing to school they seldom have sufficient time to be entrusted with the entire training of the dog, so it naturally falls to Mother.

The worst dog trainers are undoubtedly mothers with young children; they simply haven't time or energy to give to an animal. The result is the dog becomes a nuisance. It is regarded as the plaything of the children, and seldom have the children been taught to respect the privacy of the dog. It amazes me what patience most dogs show towards children. They suffer being dressed up and put in a cart, they endure their ears being pulled, and being hugged too tightly, and they endure being woken up when they want to sleep in the gentle manner of nice dogs. But I am definitely not in agreement with people who buy puppies for small children, and then abandon the puppy to the mercy of the children and feel angry if the puppy bites the children or tears up their things. Few children would stand what many puppies have to put up with, and if in time the puppy grows adult and no longer wishes to be the target for little 'Willie's' tantrums, and answers back with a bite, it is always the dog that is to blame, never the child. I can quite honestly say that when my children were tiny I never left my dogs to play with them unsupervised, in case, without meaning to be unkind, the child did something that hurt or annoyed the dog. The children were trained to 'let sleeping dogs lie', and that they must not approach a dog that was not wagging its tail happily. Most dogs seem to put up with the rough handling children give them in the same way as they put up with the nips from their own puppies. But without growling, how can a dog show it has had enough? That is why I think all small irresponsible children should be supervised in their play with dogs. Once the dog has learnt that only by growling can it check the children and their unwanted attentions, it is a short step to the quick irritable bite, and a very short step to becoming a problem dog or one on its last walk to the vet's.

Children must be trained if they are to be good companions to dogs, and that is the way round I think it should be, for the human being always has the advantage over the dog, as it is the human being who decides its destiny. I have with my own eyes seen boys and girls send their dogs after livestock. How then is the dog to know that to chase cats and chickens, not to mention sheep, is a crime? Children can quickly learn to train their small dog to quite a high standard of obedience, and love doing it. If they have a pride and personal interest in the dog they will not teach it bad ways. It is up to the parents to see this interest is cultivated.

But in this treatise children can be left out, for they are not suitable handlers of difficult dogs.

How many grown-ups make suitable handlers? I regretfully say good handlers are few and far between, the main reason being lack of light and shade in their personal character and make-up. Every day of my life I am astounded at the amount of annoyance and inconvenience owners put up with on account of their dogs. And by this I do not mean having holidays restricted by not being able to take their dog along, nor the work resulting from polished floors being covered with paw marks. I mean real good cases of having their new linoleum torn to shreds, or the baker refusing to call because the dog bites him, or not being able to turn over in bed at night because the dog bites if disturbed from his position in the centre of the bed; or not being able to knit one's husband a pullover, because the dog dislikes his mistress knitting and bites her as soon as the knitting is picked up! Or having to watch a dog chew something up because he won't let go. Or having to stay rigid in the garage because your guard dog has misunderstood whom to guard! These and countless other faults are borne by numberless owners for no other reason than that they love their dogs. I feel very humble when I read their letters, for I doubt whether I would tolerate these faults so easily.

On the other hand I get irritable with the people who try to persuade me to take their dogs from them and train them myself, for I explain that if I trained their dog it would probably take me half a day to get it trained to quite a high standard; but that the dog would return to them just as bad as ever, because they themselves would not be trained in controlling it, and that it is their voice and their manner of working the dog that matters. I explain that I worship dogs, that I have no inhibitions when I work dogs. I say silly, lovely things to them, I love them so much I can hardly keep my hands or face away from them in caress, and the problem of training them hardly ever arises for more than a few moments when we decide between ourselves who is to be master—and it most certainly is going to be me. After that it is purely a matter of showing the dog what is wanted in order to get loving and instant obedience from it. But if the owner likes to come with the dog, and honestly wishes to train it, then by copying everything I do, however silly they may think it, they have reasonable hope of having a good dog in a very short time.

Some years ago I tried out an experiment. I asked through the press for twenty-five of the worst dogs in Britain to take part in the first residential course for dogs and owners ever to be held in Britain. I wanted to prove myself right or wrong in the assumption that dogs can be trained to a high standard of obedience in a few hours. The dogs turned up with their owners; they were not all bad dogs, but a large majority were fighters, biters, pullers, won't come when called, etc. The owners hadn't all the right voices, or temperaments. Many of them found the strenuous work almost beyond them; all admitted they had no idea there was so much to learn. At the end of three days when there was nothing more I could teach them, dogs and owners passed a stiff test. There was only one failure, an Alsatian who behaved perfectly without his owner, but who would go for people if they went too near his mistress when they were together.

This guarding instinct in dogs can be dangerous, and no amount of training will stop it, unless the owner really wants to stop it, and shows great displeasure when the dog attacks. Most owners of this type of dog had grown to like being well protected. But once the instinct has been developed to this extent, the dog, in my opinion, is unreliable and therefore dangerous. Away from its owner the Alsatian was trained to a high standard and was sweet-tempered.

I spend many hours teaching TONE OF VOICE to the owners, and we had a film made at a course which clearly shows the response by the dogs to the owners' tone of voice, and then my voice. Inevitably some of the dogs came to me, not the owners, but it was fascinating to watch the steady improvement in the owners; to see them learn to let themselves go with praise when the dogs obeyed, and steadily learn to use the right firm tone in giving commands, and thus getting instant obedience. Bit by bit they got accustomed to the fact that to give a dog a very sharp jerk on a choke chain is not cruel. In fact the dogs who were depressed cheered up as soon as I jerked them firmly and confidently, secure in the knowledge that the right choke chain could not hurt them. This I demonstrated on my own wrist. Whilst I am on the subject of choke chains, far, far too many people have the wrong type. They buy the thin ones in the mistaken idea that they are kinder than the thick ones. I refuse to work a dog on a thin one, as I know it hurts the dog.

What do I do if the owner cannot get the right tone of voice? That is one of my big problems; it is a physical impossibility for many women to have a wide range of tone. If they try to get the right tone it often ends up as a squeak. This makes training doubly difficult for those people. All they can do is to train their dogs by voice and signal, and eventually work almost entirely on signal. The tone of voice coupled with sending out the right telepathic thought is most important. You would be surprised how dogs pick up thought before you have ever said a word. It is useless giving commands without willing them to obey with your mind as well.

Most women, to begin with, think the training is harsh, and find it difficult to jerk their dogs, or put them to the 'down' position. Unless they can master this over-sentimental feeling they will fail. If you learn the correct way of doing these things it is akin to ju-jutsu and in no way hurts or upsets the dog. The slow way on the other hand annoys the dog and often leads to bites. The best dog handler is the quick-minded type of person who wants to learn it all in a day. To those who say you must walk before you run in dog training, I say 'Nonsense': if you can keep up with your dog's brain there is no need to worry. I have no hesitation in saying it is inevitably the owner who is much slower to learn than the dog; and they admit it.

Very often one has to train the dog who in turn trains the owner. I have often seen a dog, on my command 'Halt', sit, whilst the owner has absentmindedly walked on, only to be brought to a standstill by the dog.

The question of age of the dog constantly crops up. Are there limits as to when one can train a dog? My answer is: any age between three months and eight years old, providing the dog is fit. After that the dog in my opinion should not be bothered by training; before that the puppy gets tired too quickly. The age of the owner matters far more. Training a dog is almost a gymnastic feat in my classes. The owner has to bend down quickly to push her dog to the sit many times in an hour. Speed in working is essential if you want your dog to work happily. Dawdlers make bad handlers. If you want your dog to walk well to heel don't wait for it; stride out, and if it doesn't keep up, jerk it quickly on and up to you using an excited tone of voice and lots of praise. The slower you go the slower the dog will go, and the more bored you both will be. Running and stopping suddenly teaches a dog to sit like lightning and become quite a game. No room here for the three hundred pounders. Dog training revitalizes owners, if done in the right spirit with others in a class, and it can be wonderful fun at home when you feel like making progress. If you feel irritable or worried don't train your dog. Train him when you and he are in a happy mood; get quick results; give quick praise, and then leave him in peace. Never nag. What can't be achieved in ten minutes will seldom be achieved in ten hours of boredom for the dog.

Some owners choose big dogs and haven't the physical strength to control them or train them. Unless these breeds are trained young few women can do anything with them. Breeds like Pyrenean mountain dogs and boxers come into this category, for they have enormous strength and will-power when adult. All dogs are best trained when young, but most dogs can be trained when adult.

Providing they get the right type of owners there are few dogs which cannot be made into reasonable companions. But I regret to say there are a vast number of misfits in this dog-owner partnership. With some I believe it is a sheer waste of time attempting to train them.

NERVES AND NEUROTIC DOGS

Hysterical dogs, biting dogs, dogs that shriek if left alone, dogs that whine and bark or shriek in cars, dogs that apparently take leave of their senses when they see another dog, and dogs that tear up everything in the house, can all be dealt with under the above heading.

Owners of these dogs must work out for themselves under which subheading their own dog is classified.

Hysterical dogs can be the result of inbreeding, or purely of mating together parents with the wrong temperaments. When the puppy first comes to its new owner it is probably a tiny mite and the mistress of its destiny pours out all her mother love, and sympathizes with its fears; it is taken everywhere with her, or someone stays at home to make it feel it is not deserted. Most probably it is allowed the luxury of sleeping under the eiderdown of its new owner's bed, because it is so tiny and helpless, and its cries are so pathetic.

If it is a small dog its fear of traffic is overcome by being carried in the town, its unwillingness to walk amongst big feet is sympathized with by the owner who uses endearing words of encouragement to help it take its first steps in this big terrifying world of traffic and feet. The result is the puppy gains no self-confidence, it is all boosted confidence given to it by the owner using comforting words and carrying it. Should one ever try to give the dog confidence by firm jerks and a confident happy voice, paying no attention to it sitting down and refusing to walk, then one is bound to meet the oversentimental, and ill-educated, so-called dog lover, who will in a loud voice accuse you of being cruel to a tiny puppy. Few owners can retaliate in public, so the best thing to do is to ignore such people and carry on with what you are doing, in the knowledge that only by ignoring the puppy's fears will you help it to overcome them. Walk firmly on, speaking happily to the puppy or nervous dog, making it come on with quick jerks, and very soon you will have helped it over its first hurdle, fear. I cure many dogs that will not show themselves at dog shows owing to nerves; dogs that will not be handled by men; dogs that are terrified of bangs and such-like noises. The nervous show dog is easy. In most cases all it needs is a choke chain, a long lead, and a few quick sharp jerks when it sits back fearfully. That, coupled with a confident happy tone of voice and plenty of love when he comes on, soon does the trick. Being a show dog it has probably never worn a choke chain for fear of spoiling its ruff or hair round its neck, or some such beauty points; secondly the owner has never obedience-trained it for fear it will sit in the show ring instead of standing. But in omitting obedience training the owner has forgotten it is just as easy to teach a dog to stand, as it is to sit, and that is part of the training curriculum. Obedience training of some sort should be given to all dogs whether they be show dogs or just household pets.

Why should dogs be allowed to dislike or be more frightened of men than of women, unless the dog has at some time or other been frightened or ill-treated by a man? I think it is more often a ruse by the dog to get more attention from its lady owner. Subconsciously she may also dislike the opposite sex and finds that their mutual dislike is rather comforting, although she may believe she wants it otherwise, for dogs pick up one's mental thoughts more than physical reactions. I have through constant contact with animals picked up this sort of radar communication, and how often have I picked up the owner's thoughts which are in direct contradiction to her actions? How often have I seen the owner annoyed when I have told her what I have picked up, and told her I don't think she really wants the dog to be friendly with men. What is the answer to this problem? The answer is you must make the dog go and talk to men. Pay not the slightest attention when it cringes or sits back, and won't be stroked. Don't at first expect it to like it or endure it happily. In my opinion unless the dog is a show one there is no point whatsoever in making dogs like anyone they don't want to know, but if that is the owner's wish so must it be.

The first thing to do is to love and pet your dog, then hold it quite firmly by the choke chain, give the command 'Talk', and ask the man to stroke its head and scratch its chest. Next give him the lead and ask him to take it for a short walk, jerking it on if it won't go, then when he returns praise it for all you are worth. I think it is rather cruel to force a dog to be sociable to someone it doesn't like, but all dogs should be taught to allow themselves to be handled on the command 'Stand', in case the vet has to examine the dog. So the sooner it learns this exercise the better. But I fail to understand why people complain that their dog will not be friends with strangers. Who wants a dog to be friendly with strangers? As long as it is polite and well-behaved surely that is enough? If however you have a show dog the judge is always impressed by a nice happy friendly dog; he hates risking being bitten by a nervous dog. Bad temperament should be heavily penalized so that owners are not encouraged to breed with it and pass on this fault. If an adult dog shows nerves what good is he as a sire? However many beauty points he may possess, he can never be a first-class dog.

Some of the saddest letters I get come from wives with dogs that dislike their husbands; dogs that even go so far as to bite the husband apparently without any specific reason. The cause I think is jealousy.

What would I do with them? I would train the dog and the husband to respect each other's likes and dislikes. I would train the dog to go instantly to its basket and stay there when the husband is about. I would never allow it to lie in front of the fire and bite the husband when he moves his feet, which is a very common complaint. I would ask the husband to feed the dog, and if possible never feed it myself, for most animals can be won over through their tummies. And lastly I would ask the husband to ignore the dog's lack of affection and not try to force himself on the dog, however much it offends his dignity not to be liked. Very often when you ignore a dog it makes the first advances.

Once more I stress the fact you cannot make an animal love you, it must come naturally. Many dogs are 'one man' or 'one woman' dogs and do not want the love or companionship of any other human being.

However, should the dog show its dislike of the husband or children by seriously biting them, then I think that dog should be put to sleep. No child's safety is worth risking for any dog; and although the dog can be kept away from them both, that is no life for a family dog, or the dog owner.

The best cure for a biting dog is to have a long piece of string attached to its choke chain. When it attempts to bite, the person it goes for should pick up the string and suspend the dog for a few seconds off its front legs, leaving its back feet on the ground, and at the same time by using a thunderous tone of voice should make it very clear to the dog that its actions are quite unwarranted, and in no way going to be tolerated.

The dog whilst suspended thus will feel like choking and will quickly realize who is master of the situation. But how many children, or husbands for that matter, are capable of carrying out this unpleasant treatment? Very few. Therefore, as the dog does not love or respect them, why keep it? I can never understand people who ring me up and ask my advice on what to do with a dog that has seriously bitten a child more than once. My answer must always be that that dog is a beastly minded dog, so why take the risk of injury to your family? Obviously the owner is incapable of training it or it would never have reached this state of retaliation. For dogs are only driven to bite under such circumstances because they despise people—the result of not having been trained by them to do anything interesting or useful.

Boredom is another problem I have to tackle in dogs. These days they have little to interest them, beyond the daily walks which are often only to the shops and back, not the woods and fields. Anyway the woods and fields are mostly empty of exciting smells and things to chase. The result is that dogs like corgis and spaniels with a background of useful work become neurotic, and as they can't hunt or chase anything they bite their owners. These self-same dogs, given a fixed schedule of obedience work or even just household tricks to perform, become different characters. Unfortunately these days owners are so busy that the time taken to train a dog can hardly be spared. They hope that the dog will fit in with their household arrangements without any special training, except house manners. They get annoyed or disappointed when this is not so. The result is that the dog becomes neurotic and sometimes vicious.

Every dog, like every child, should have some routine work given it to do every day, even if only for ten minutes a day. If the dog continues to be vicious after you have trained it, there is something lacking or abnormal in its make-up, and abnormal dogs cannot safely be kept. But this does not mean the dog should be given away to a so-called 'kind home in the country' to bite other unsuspecting people. I think the owner should face up to his or her responsibility and put it to sleep, and also face up to the fact that the owner has failed the dog, and vow to learn more about dogs before having another.

Bangs and noises that terrify dogs are a constant source of trouble to dog owners. Fireworks can cause a night of terror for dog and owner. So may be a walk in the town or country when a backfire may make the dog slip its lead and disappear for hours or even for ever.

How is the owner to blame for this state of affairs? The answer is that familiarity breeds contempt, and if the owner takes the trouble to make these noises quite familiar to the dog during the day, the dog will soon ignore them, or even enjoy them. I trained Juno, my former Great Dane, who was a shivering mass of terrors when I bought her, to love gun-fire. I had a toy pistol with caps and played with it as a game, fired it and said 'Attack' and had a rough and tumble game with her. Soon she connected the game with the bang and became used to it and enjoyed it. Then if anyone fired a gun she looked too beautiful, obviously longing to go and attack or have a game. I used also to drop heavy books unexpectedly, and then I praised her and laughed with her; dogs love laughter and smiles like children do. I always clapped my hands when she did right and she soon connected clapping with my happy voice and smiling face. If you make odd bangs and noises at intervals your dog will soon forget its fear.

One of the most difficult vices to overcome is that of the dog who will not be left alone. This takes longer to cure than most faults, because it is the owner who must be cured—of lack of firmness. Daily firmness is essential. The dog must be taught to lie down and stay down. When it gets up the owner must return to it and sound cross with it, and put it down again. There must be no let-up on this. It must be made to stay down in spite of piercing shrieks or whines. It may be necessary to give it a firm jerk as it is put 'down' on the choke chain. If it barks give the command 'Cease'—and mean it. Tone of voice is everything in this case. Occasionally I have found the words 'Shut up' extremely effective if snapped out. There must be no pleading with the dog to stay, for that won't help. But when it does stay, even for a few minutes, the praise must be terrific.

Always remember dogs cannot bark for long lying down, they get tired. Therefore whenever it makes a nuisance of itself by barking make it lie down. This is quite the most important exercise in dog training. If necessary you must sit down on a chair and put the dog with its lead on into the down position on the floor beside you. Then run the lead under the arch of your shoe. If the dog attempts to get up, give the command 'Down' and tighten the lead by pulling it upwards from where it runs under your shoe. By this method the dog's head is pulled gently to the ground, and it must sooner or later lie down unless it wishes to choke itself. Try not to have to bend down yourself; it is better that the dog shouldn't connect you with what is going on. When it does lie down say something nice to it and show you are pleased, but not in an excited tone of voice or it will get up again. When the exercise is over then give it real petting.

Do this exercise for a few minutes to start with, eventually sitting the dog down for half an hour. Never relent whilst doing this exercise. Remember that if the dog obeys the pulling lead the choke chain will immediately release itself, so it is within the dog's power to be comfortable. I cannot repeat too often that to make a problem dog good you must have a strong will. Let the dog win and you are further back than when you started.

Leave the dog in the 'down' position for longer periods at a time each day. When he trusts that you are going to come back, the trouble of never being able to leave him alone in the house does not occur. Smacking is useless, scolding is only a little better. It is the quiet firmness that wins, never failing to put him back and down where he came from. Occasionally a 'put on' cross voice will steady a nervous dog, but never lose your temper. This exercise is just as much a test of the owner's character as the dog's. Weak people never win. Remember this trouble is probably your fault in the first place; it is up to you to put it right.

Always do everything you can to make the exercise liked by the dog. Give it its favourite blanket to lie on, especially in the car; if possible let it have its own chair in the sitting-room. It is only when all these things fail that sterner measures have to be taken. And remember problem dogs need far sterner measures than puppies or normal nice dogs.

Now let's deal with dogs that tear things up. In adult male dogs I have no hesitation in saying I believe it is sex trouble. Castrate the dog is my solution. It is useless letting him mate with an occasional bitch, that only makes him much worse. With boxers in particular, many of those that tear things up will be found to be 'monorchids', which means they have only one testicle descended. This sexual abnormality makes them destructive. Castration is difficult in these cases and an operation to find the undescended testicle has to be carried out before castration can take place. Dachshunds also seem very prone to this trouble, but without exception I have found that castration will cure these destructive urges. But it takes two or three months for the operation to have full effect.

There is a prejudice against this operation in some circles, but I am sure that such people would change their minds if they followed the careers of difficult dogs which have been so treated. I have recommended castration for a vast number of dogs with certain vices, and in every case the owners have been most satisfied with the results. The dogs have in no way been spoilt nor run to fat, nor have they lost a lively character. It helps to stop a dog that fights. It makes the lamp-post to lamp-post trek a thing of the past, for the dog returns to the squatting position for passing urine. It stops that eternal search after the on-heat bitch. And it also stopped a pekinese from lifting its leg over the wall-paper, the result of having been trained to use newspaper as a puppy! Dogs only get fat through overfeeding. Undoubtedly castrated dogs need less food when so treated, as they worry less over distractions, and bitches. They are also much nicer companions out on a walk as they pay less attention to smells and they tolerate other dogs in the same house much better. It is an old wives' tale that other dogs attack them; you will find that other dogs ignore them. I can give the addresses of the many people who own these dogs, and if anyone has doubts I am sure these owners would be pleased to show you their dogs or write to you about them.

I think far too many dogs are over-sexed, and would lead happier lives without the trouble of possessing the sex they are never going to use. If wandering mongrels were castrated there would be fewer of those poor little puppies sold in markets, which eventually end up in homes for lost dogs. The road accidents caused by dogs would also be greatly decreased, for it is the mongrels not the show dogs that are the chief cause.

Some vets won't castrate dogs. They can't in my opinion have had much experience of the results. I have had a great deal, and wouldn't dream of recommending it if I did not think it has been a good thing for the cases I mention. Before recommending that any male dog should be put to sleep for vice, I always try castration. In many cases it has saved the dog's life.

To sum up this section on nervous dogs, I recommend some form of training and work in all cases. I believe the owner must consistently display firmness and patience. I implore breeders to stop breeding bad temperaments.

BUMPTIOUS DOGS

Dogs that jump up in a wild frenzy of joy at meeting all human beings seem to cause great trouble to countless owners. 'How can I stop my dog greeting strangers like old friends?' is a common letter I get. Which leads to the more serious aspect of how to teach a dog to guard the home and person of its owner.

We must of course divide this question into two parts: the behaviour of puppies, and that of adult dogs.

Dealing first of all with puppies, I would much rather see and meet an over friendly puppy than one that slinks away shivering and shaking when strangers come to the house, for it is the shivery and shaky ones that may eventually be the cowardly biters of the future.

Nobody wants his dog to jump up causing stockings to run or leaving paw marks on the dresses and suits of everyone it meets, but it is well within the power of any owner to teach a dog to drop into the 'down' position instantly on command, and it is of course the answer to the over-eager approach to all strangers. But in teaching a young dog this, one must not make him feel it is wrong to go barking to the door when strangers come, or he will never learn to guard the house.

I believe the correct attitude to take is this: when the bell rings at the front door the householder with a young dog should put on his most excited tone of voice and rush to the door saying, 'Who is it? See 'em off!' so that the dog barks in excitement. Next, as you approach the door to open it, give the command 'Wait'. If you have trained your dog my way he will know that this means 'Stand and stay standing where you are.' To teach this, put the dog on his lead attached to the end of which should be a seven-pound kitchen scales weight, and suddenly, when walking, give the command 'Wait' and at the same time drop the lead to the ground. The dog quickly gets used to being checked by word and weight and soon learns what he must do to get the praise he waits for when he's done right. Now this lesson comes in useful, for he will not go further to greet the strangers or friends until released with the words 'Good boy, or girl' as the case may be. If your friends are dog lovers your dog will probably come in for some friendly pats as he obediently stands there, and you will get the reputation of owning a well-trained dog. If this exercise presents difficulty to you, you haven't practised enough; if the dog drags the seven-pound weight after your leaving him at the stand, use the fourteen-pound one. Never allow a dog to defeat you in anything you wish to do.

Your dog is so delighted to meet and greet all the world and his wife because you, the owner, are not his 'be all and end all'. You have not trained enough or given him enough to think about. You may even belong to the brigade who turn their dogs out into the garden for exercise, which in my opinion is fatal to a really faithful dog, training to be a guard dog.

Your dog must as far as possible always be with you in all you do, you must be indispensable to him. That is why two dogs together in one household are never so easy to train; they do not depend on their owner for everything, and may not care whether the owner comes or goes. These are the dogs most likely to greet everyone as friends as they have no real allegiance to anyone.

Some time back I got a letter from a farmer who complained that he had four or five Alsatians to guard his poultry farm and that they wouldn't guard, that they were unreliable with his wife, and didn't seem to care twopence whether he or his family existed or not. 'Yet,' he complained, 'I have one in my office on its lead when I am there.' He wanted to know how to train them really to guard and if necessary attack intruders. I think he expected me to write back with detailed instructions out of the Police Manual on Dog Training if there is such a book, but instead I asked him what affection he gave those dogs. Did he ever take them for lovely walks, or play with a ball with them? Why, I asked him, was the one in his office tied up on a lead? Surely if he loved and petted his dogs they would want to be near him and not have to be tied up near him. I assured him that guard dogs don't have to be taught to guard their owner and his property; if the dog loves you it is the most natural thing in the world for it to guard you.

I had no reply to my letter and as usual forgot what I thought was another ungrateful correspondent, but four months later I had one of the happiest possible letters from him enclosing some charming snaps of two of the dogs playing on the lawn with his wife, and two others sitting obediently in the background. His letter made me very happy, for it said the dogs were now completely different animals. He had taken my advice and given them much affection, he and his wife had taken them for walks, and trained them in obedience and above all played with them. Their suspicious natures had left them and he didn't think any thief or intruder would have a happy time. This man had the erroneous idea that you mustn't make a friend of a guard dog, that they must be more or less chained up, or left on their own, or they became soft and wouldn't do the job they were supposed to do. How wrong he was. Why, even the police dogs live at their handlers' homes and although they do not live in the house they are very much one of the family. And they are gentle creatures, not ferocious animals that in the interest of safety have to be kept away from human beings unless tracking and catching criminals.

Many people write to me to know, will I train their guard dog for them? or where can they send it to be trained for such work? I assure them that they themselves must train the dog or it will guard the person who has trained it; dogs are not machines that can be switched over at will and know whom they have to guard.

It is far more difficult to untrain a guard dog than to train it. Any handler of such a dog will tell you that the biggest problem is to teach a dog to stop attacking on command rather than to teach it to do so.

People want to know what breed of dog is best for this job, and when I tell them my little miniature English Toy Terrier weighing under ten pounds is a dog I would be perfectly safe with they think I am joking. It isn't always the biggest breed of dog that makes the best guard dog. Some of the small breeds, by their yapping alone would be adequate protection. Naturally a big dog frightens an intruder, and few unwanted visitors would face a Great Dane, purely and simply because of its size and tremendous bark. There is no special breed to choose for guarding your property and person: there are fool dogs in all breeds who would happily go off with the burglar and never look back at their homes. But that comes from lack of training by the owner. When a dog has been the constant companion of the family and has received adequate obedience training, it instinctively guards and stays at home.

If you wish to train your dog to attack on command and stop attacking on command you must do it in the right way. First, make up some padding for your right arm, and fix it on firmly. Then, in a very excited tone of voice, say 'Attack' and have a terrific tussle with the dog pulling on the padded arm, turning the whole thing into a wonderful game. Next you make the dog sit and stay and run off a few yards, each time suddenly shouting 'Attack'. The dog now knows what this means and races after you: you let him savage the padded arm for a while, then give him the command 'Leave' and make him sit or lie down. Next you must have the help of a friend. The friend must run off wearing the padded sleeve, and you must give the command 'Attack' to the dog. He must be allowed to reach the friend and have a real tussle for a few times to make him enjoy it and get really interested. Then you must put him on a cord and before he reaches the friend you must shout 'Leave'. If the dog doesn't stop, give a terrific jerk on the cord, if possible facing the dog round to you, and repeat the command 'Leave, sit', and when he does so, praise him. This training must not be overdone, it must be fun for the dog, but the dog must never become too ferocious. The idea is not to teach him to bite but to hold, therefore he must be taught 'to hold and to leave' on the padded arm as an exercise. Only in the very beginning should he be allowed to bite and pull at it to awaken his interest.

Next of course the dog must be taught to bark on command, as it is the barking that really frightens an intruder—few private owners' dogs ever get the chance of a real criminal chase. To teach a dog to bark you do several things. Get someone to knock on the door and rush to it barking yourself and using a very excited tone of voice. Then have a stick and threaten the dog, urging it to bark at you, and to cease barking as soon as you lower the stick. Next point a toy gun at it and fire the gun at the dog, also urging it to bark and later attack the hand that holds the toy gun.

Running away and letting the dog chase you is the greatest fun for the dog, and that is a most important part of his training as a guard dog. As I have previously mentioned in this book the guarding instinct in some breeds can be a menace, and the dog becomes unsafe to take with you in public places. That is why I think an ordinary householder should not train his dog to be a guard dog: it takes an experienced handler to control a really trained guard dog, and an inexperienced handler will probably find himself in court, and his dog with an order against it to be kept under control.

If the right attitude has been trained into your dog it will guard.

The question of how to make it less friendly towards strangers is a difficult one, because in general people adore it when dogs run up to them and wag their tails and show pleasure at meeting them, when really they should give the dog a scolding and even possibly a quick slap and send it back to its owner. But one never gets the co-operation of the public. I find some of them a menace: if they see a trained dog standing outside a shop, they will not leave it alone, they allow their children to hug or pet it in spite of the fact that the dog shows no interest, and gives them no welcome, and, what is worse, if you ask them to leave the dog in peace they are rude or say 'Why shouldn't we pet dogs if we love them?' My reply to that is, 'If you were a real dog lover you wouldn't torture strange dogs with your unwanted attentions.' I point out to them that my trained dogs have interest in only one person, their mistress, and they only tolerate without biting the unwanted stroking because they are polite well-trained dogs.

Very often these unwelcome attentions from the public will cause a nervous dog to get up and run away, and if it got killed or caused an accident those strangers would be responsible. But again you must have the help of friends if you wish to train your dogs not to welcome strangers. You must ask people to call at your house and when the dog rushes out to greet them they must give it a harsh word, or a quick slap if it really persists in forcing its attentions on them and send it off. I know it is a horrid thing to have to do with a friendly dog, but it is for its own sake.

Train your dog thoroughly in the two commands 'Down' and 'Leave' and he will not annoy visitors. Teach him that the command 'Talk' means he should go up to strangers and allow himself to be petted, and then you will really have a nice well-behaved dog. Teaching a dog the command 'Talk' simply means taking him up to people and asking them to caress and speak to him, whilst you are praising and reassuring him all the time. It is amazing how quickly they learn.

Personally I do not wish my dogs to be friendly with all and sundry. They tolerate politely all advances made to them and on the command 'Talk' will politely wag their tails, but that is as far as it goes, they are my dogs and mine alone.

ROAMING DOGS

How irritating it must be never to know where your dog is! Or to own a dog that perpetually wishes to go off on its own pursuits.

How does this happen? It comes about for many reasons. The first is that many people imagine it is cruel to confine a dog to the house with you, and that dogs can't be happy without their freedom. It comes about because people own dogs and haven't the time to exercise them, or the time to look after them, and they take the easiest way out by opening the front door and letting their dogs go out on their own, knowing they will return when tired or hungry.

These people lack imagination, they do not visualize what might happen in those hours the dog is running free on its own pursuits. They never think that their dog may cause a human being to die in a car accident, nor do they visualize the dog getting injured and lying uncared for on the road. They have never thought that their male dog may mate with some tiny little uncared for bitch on heat and cause her to suffer or die having puppies too big for her. They do not think of the risk of their dog picking up infection. All they like is to have a dog to bark at intruders at night and to play occasionally with the children. They have no idea what they miss. They do not know what heights of intelligence can be reached by a dog. They should never own a dog, a cat would suit them better, for cats prefer being allowed to roam when the spirit moves them, and most cat lovers agree that it is not kind to confine a cat too closely, although I think cats would also miss the deep affection this type of owner never bestows on an animal.

How can one cure a roaming dog? First of all by training. Any sort of work makes a dog more interested in its owner. Having the dog with you when you shop, when you go in the car, when you are in the home, all tend to make the dog rely on you for all his needs. But there are some male dogs tortured by the sex urge and if there is a bitch on heat within five miles I have heard owners complain their dog knows and is a menace. My answer to that is, castrate him.

The roaming instinct is also the reason why the dogs do not come to their owners' call when out for exercise. This is a major problem and a large percentage of my correspondence is about it. The owners often say the dog is good and obedient in the house or garden, but get it outside where smells abound, or other dogs roam, and the dog becomes completely deaf to orders. What can they do?

They must put their dog on a long lead and a choke chain and take it where there are plenty of distractions, leave it at the sit and walk away from the dog to the fullest extent of the lead. Give the command 'Come' prefacing all commands with the dog's name; if the dog looks about elsewhere or doesn't literally leap to its feet to obey, give it a very sharp jerk towards you and when it comes love it for all you are worth. The whole training depends on the way you jerk. The choke chain running end must be under the dog's chin, for in this way the jerk comes on the top of the neck—which is very muscular—and couldn't possibly cause any injury or pain to the dog; but it *does* give the dog a shock, and I have known poodles and similar nervous dogs to give a squeal. This is not pain but shock, and you must carry on: the dog will soon learn that if it comes quickly it gets much love and praise, if it doesn't come quickly it gets an almighty jerk and has to come anyway. I reckon it only takes a few minutes to teach a dog to come when called.

Occasionally a very tough stubborn dog will not learn this way, and then once more you have to have co-operation from a friend who should if possible have a dog with her. She should have a spare long leather lead in her hand, and when your dog comes up to her dog and won't return to you when you call, she should give it a crack with the leather lead over its backside and say 'Go Back' in a horrid tone of voice. The owner should meanwhile be calling in her most endearing tone of voice, and there is soon no doubt at all in the dog's mind which is the best place. I find this is easily taught in class in an enclosed field, because when there are twenty or more pupils all willing to help the owner whose dog won't come when called, by slapping it with a leather lead if it comes their way, the dog finds it most unpleasant to be away from its owner and safety. I hate having to do this to disobedient dogs, but these measures have to be meted out to dogs who don't love their owners. For make no mistake, if your dog doesn't come when called you take only second place in his mind to smells or other dogs. Otherwise the old trick of calling him and running away from him would be effective. He would think you were going to leave him and he would love you so much he would not want you out of his sight, and would run after you. You could then give the command 'Sit' and catch him. No, if your dog does not come it means he doesn't respect you, and without respect you have no true love from your dog.

Force in any form is repulsive to many dog owners, and I heartily agree with them. I often have to use these more forceful measures to teach the dogs obedience to their unloved owners, and I also feel revolted at having to do it, but it is my duty to help train these dogs, and if the dogs couldn't care less whether their owners jumped into the sea or not what can one do? I always find these dogs will come instantly to my call, which is very annoying for the owners, but then I am sending out by telepathy not only the 'or else' message, but my tremendous faith in them and my deep love for them when they behave well. Too many owners try to catch their dogs when they approach. I tell them to raise their hands up to their own chests and not use them menacingly to grab their dogs. Without the hands waving about the dogs will come right up close to the owner's knees and should sit on command, when the owners can drop down and kiss and love them for coming. I can't tell owners often enough that dogs love being kissed, they adore contact with the human face.

Should titbits ever be given to a dog on returning to its owner?

With a puppy I think so, and occasionally with an adult dog, but not as a rule, or the dog may get fed up and go off again when you have nothing to give one day.

The right firm tone of voice when the command 'Come' is given, the immense show of love when the dog comes, and the more severe measures recommended if the dog is a stubborn one—those are the only methods I use to teach countless dogs to return instantly to their owners.

MISFITS

So far in this chapter I have been pretty confident that with sensible obedience training by willing and co-operative owners practically every fault in dogs can be cured. Now I want to discuss what happens when this dog-owner partnership can only be called a misfit. There are hundreds of misfits for whom I see little hope of cure.

The most difficult to help are the elderly owners, either man or woman, who for purely physical reasons cannot carry out the necessary corrections. Many of them have arthritis in their joints, which makes them weak in the wrists, or makes bending down to put the dog to the sit almost an impossibility. Yet they love their dogs and are often the keenest of learners. Is it fair that they should have to put up with disobedient dogs, or is there some way of helping them train their dogs? Yes, there is. For example, when teaching a dog to lie down I usually use two methods. In one I put the dog to the sit, and standing in front of it, I lift one leg and push the opposite shoulder, which puts the dog off its balance and down it goes without fuss. Or when walking I catch hold of the running end of the choke chain underneath the chin and pull it quickly to the ground slightly ahead of the dog's chin. Then a quick press on the dog's flank with the other hand completes the movement and down goes the dog, again without fuss if done swiftly enough. Now it is quite obvious that these exercises could not be easily carried out by elderly or infirm people. Yet this 'down' exercise is wanted for the cure of almost every vice, for at the 'down' you have your dog under your control. Well, this exercise can be done just as easily by placing the left foot over the lead when you are standing up so that the lead runs under the arch of your shoe. Then pull quickly and strongly on the lead, and the dog's head is pulled to the down, and it quickly lies down to get more comfortable.

To teach a dog to sit on command it is not necessary to use the left hand to push the dog down. It can just as well be done by working the dog against a wall on the left-hand side so that it cannot sidle away from you, and then with the firm command 'Sit' give the dog's rump a tap with a rolled-up newspaper or the end of another leather lead which you have in your hand. It is the noise that makes the dog sit, not any pain caused by the tap. If the dog shows signs of biting, as some nasty dogs do when put to the down, muzzle them for one or two minutes; they will soon find out that they cannot bite and must go down, and that directly they have gone into the down position they get praise, and then all idea of biting in retaliation will be given up. Be sure when making a dog sit that the lead, which is always held in the right hand for training purposes, is raised tightly over the right hip, for that almost puts a dog in the sitting position without further help.

Pulling on the lead can seldom be cured by infirm people because the dog needs a really quick sharp jerk to correct it. It is for this reason that I do not recommend big dogs or heavy boisterous dogs for old people. Even if they get some young person, or the trainer at a club, to do the initial pulling, the dog will soon realize it has its elderly owner at its mercy and start pulling again.

One thing can be done, however. Take the dog's lead in your left hand and whilst walking with it, turn sharply, throwing the right leg in front of the dog's nose and turning to the left all the time. The dog is checked quickly because otherwise it would bump into that right leg and it won't bump into the leg more than once or twice before it realizes it is safer to keep back. Always use the word 'heel' as you turn. Association of ideas lies beneath the whole system of training: that, and the praise the dog gets when it does right.

I cannot stress too strongly that an owner who is frightened of his dog must protect himself if he wishes to train it. If you know your dog will bite when you try to make it lie down, naturally you are sending out fear waves, and the dog knows you are beaten and will bite all the more. If however you have protected your hands by thick leather gloves, you can with confidence ignore the efforts of the dog to bite, and what is better retaliate with two or three good jerks on its choke chain. Unfortunately nobody can teach your dog to respect *you*. They can teach the dog the exercise, so that it knows what to do, but you yourself must carry out that exercise with confidence, secure in the knowledge that the dog cannot hurt you. Then and only then will the dog obey you happily. As soon as the dog obeys, cast away your protection, and have confidence that you will not be bitten. Directly the dog has been put down, scratch its chest, for no dog will bite when you are scratching its chest, it is a movement that calms the fiercest breast.

I don't believe timid people make good trainers. I don't believe oversentimental people make good trainers, as with any problem dog there is bound to be friction at one time or another until the dog recognizes who is master. If you feel quite sick at having to jerk a dog on its choke chain you will not do it with vigour, you will therefore nag at the dog with ineffectual jerks which would never train a dog, and both you and it are getting nowhere. If you take a dog to a training school undoubtedly you get help. I do all the initial jerks necessary to save the owner and the dog from misunderstandings, but the owner must keep up to the high standard reached in class when the class is over. If you do not, the dog becomes cunning and behaves like a lamb in class, only to throw off the cloak of goodness later on. I well remember a lady who had just won the obedience certificate at a dog show being pulled like nothing on earth down the street, shouting at me as she passed at her dog's speed, 'What price my future obedience champion?' Personally I wouldn't have tolerated such behaviour, but she thought it funny. And that brings me to another aspect of training dogs. So many people think their naughty dogs are really rather funny. If they think that, there is no hope for them or their dogs, as they do not really object to the dog's faults.

You must really want to make your dog good, you must put everything you have got into teaching him kindly but quickly to obey. If one day you rock with laughter at his having eaten your knitting, and roar with rage the next day when it is your Sunday hat, how is the dog to know what you will tolerate and what you won't? I don't tolerate destruction of any kind; if one day you allow him to play with your old gloves how is he to know the difference when he finds your new gloves and tears them up?

Quite the most difficult thing to teach owners is enthusiasm. How dry and dull I find lots of them; they don't seem to be terribly pleased when the dog does right, it doesn't seem to matter much when the dog does wrong, and the result is a sort of grey picture with no light or shade. The dog also becomes grey in nature, it does its training with its tail down, it yawns as it stays resignedly at the sit or down, and eventually it refuses to do anything well, it is happy in its mediocrity. I hate that; I like to appear very angry when the dog does wrong, although curiously enough I never feel angry with the dogs. I like to bubble over with joy when they do right. I know I must look a perfect ass when training dogs, a cross between a ballet dancer and a clown, for I am always on the move. I try not to let the dogs feel bored for a second whilst that particular exercise is being carried out, and I always have a quick romp with each one after every exercise. I shall be sorry when I become too old to feel like this, for in spite of the fact that one pupil remarked that my classes were more like the Palladium than a dog class, I do believe that enthusiasm in working both dogs and owners is essential for success. How I hate to see dogs and owners ploughing round a hall with the trainer issuing orders which many owners don't comprehend or carry out. How I hate the idea that if a dog fails on something it cannot have another chance because of shortage of time. That is why I find my week-end courses so satisfying. I have all day to cure the dogs' and owners' faults, no one grumbles if I spent twenty minutes on one dog and then win, for that is what we are there for—to make sure no dog leaves with the faults it came with. I think they are as anxious as I am that the dog should be good. There is a great camaraderie amongst owners of difficult dogs, and if we all pull together we must win.

So often in the street I feel like snatching a pulling dog from its owner, correcting it, and giving it back. One day I was walking behind a very troublesome dog with its owner and heard her say to it, 'If you don't behave I shall take you to Mrs. Woodhouse.' I never let on that the threat could easily have been carried out sooner than the dog anticipated!

Sometimes the training or correction of the dog in the home is impossible because the husband or wife or some other relative doesn't approve of the training and deliberately spoils the dog or lets it get away with doing wrong because he thinks it cruel to train dogs, or rather enjoys seeing the dog do naughty things in the same way as 'Boys will be boys'. Then there is the opposite type who imagines himself a smashing dog trainer. He doesn't need anyone to show him what to do, he thunders at the dog, and gets poor results, then out of pique suggests the best cure for naughty dogs is to sell them, give them away, or put them down. This causes great rifts in families, and I shudder to think of the number of divorces or quarrels dogs have caused in the past. I well remember the husband of one person I met who had shouted at her 'Get rid of that dog or I go.' 'That is easily answered,' said the wife, 'go'. Many a quarrel is caused by differences of opinion as to whether the dog shall live in the house or a kennel. Whether the dog shall sleep on the bed or in its basket. Whether the wife can accompany the husband on an outing where dogs cannot go. All these rows could be avoided if the dog were trained, for a trained dog does not need a baby sitter, a trained dog sleeps in its own bed, a trained dog makes no mess or trouble in a house, so the kennel plan never comes into operation.

Lots of dogs are sick in cars. This is not a physical defect but a training defect: the dog is not accustomed to the movement of a car and does not trust its owner enough to rest assured that no harm will come to it. With training, a dog relaxes under all circumstances, and its sickness disappears. That is why chains on cars, or pills from the vet seldom effect a cure, whilst training will. Once a dog has been taught to lie down and ignore all distractions, and to have faith that its owner will return in due course, that dog relaxes in a car. Put its own familiar bedding on the back seat, and it needs no further attention. Always take a puppy a lot in a car from an early age, a grown-up dog does not adjust itself to motion so quickly. I once took my two dogs on a Silver City plane to Belfast and left them in the car. In spite of the terrific noise and vibrations they were perfectly calm and happy. In fact I felt much worse than they did as I don't like flying; they trusted Mistress and knew no fear.

Fear so often causes dogs to be 'Difficult Dogs': they wet the carpets, just as children wet their beds, normal house training breaks down and desperate owners write to me for new training methods. All that is wanted to right the trouble is to give the dog confidence. Put it in the kitchen where the floor can be washed, praise the dog when you greet it in the morning, completely ignoring the puddle, give only one meal early in the day and restrict drinking after 5 p.m., and in most cases the trouble clears up. The poor dog knows it has done wrong to puddle, even the tiniest puppy learns quickly what is right or wrong. Add to the dog's fear when it has made a mistake and you will never cure the fault. I have known a night or two with the owner in their bedroom to cure this fault completely, for the dog rests peacefully. Dogs undoubtedly suffer night terrors if they are highly strung, and develop all sorts of queer faults, yet these faults have been found to disappear on holiday when the dog has been with you day and night. I always believe dogs are like small children, and well I remember lying awake as a small child on Nanny's day out suffering tortures for fear she might get run over by a bus, and not until she came home did I fall asleep. I think the same thing happens with beloved highly strung dogs: the night is long for them, where they cannot hear their owner, and they sleep restlessly and then their bladder plays them up and a puddle results. Think before you punish a dog that has been perfectly clean in the past.

QUARRELSOME DOGS

Jealous dogs, fighting dogs, growling dogs, nervous dogs all come into this category of quarrelsome dogs. They can cause complete misery in any household. I know of one household that owns two dogs, one a Staffordshire bull terrier, and one a charming old fox terrier. The two dogs belong respectively to the husband and wife, but never the twain shall meet, for the Staffordshire has only one idea in its head and that is to annihilate the old-age pensioner and reign supreme alone in that household. He only developed this hatred for the fox terrier when he grew up. As a puppy he was all right. What should the owners do to make life liveable with two dogs, neither of which they wish to part with? I feel that as this situation has been allowed to develop over quite a long period of time, no very practical training has been carried out. The easiest way out has been taken by separating the dogs and dividing the household in two. I would give the bull terrier a course of obedience training, and take it out and about to meet other dogs as often as possible. I would fix up a very strong chain and collar near its bed or basket and make it lie down and stay down in that whenever the two members of the family wish to be in that room with the fox terrier. If the dog growled or showed signs of jealous temper I would jerk it hard on the choke chain giving simultaneously the command 'Leave'. Then I would pet it. I would take the dogs out together on leads with the bull terrier wearing temporarily a greyhound type of muzzle. No possible damage could then occur to the old dog, and I believe that by enjoying their walks together they would become friendly. I would never pet one in front of the other without speaking lovingly to them both. I have trained some terrible fighters to lie peacefully beside each other and see no reason why these two dogs cannot be made to tolerate, if not to love, each other. One often hears of spaniels, especially mother and daughter, who so hate each other that one has to be put to sleep to gain peace. This is terribly sad, and, on the part of the owner, an admission of failure to teach them obedience. You cannot make them love each other, any more than I can teach dogs to love their owners, but you can teach them to ignore each other by successful obedience training. The same sort of thing arises when people get a new kitten or puppy. How can they train the other animal to tolerate and accept it? This is not a very difficult problem if the newcomer is small enough to confine in an indoor kennel or cage at night, with the old dog chained to his bed near the newcomer, for I have found that when animals share the night in close proximity to each other they seldom are at war afterwards. Again, of course, the old well-known command 'Leave' comes into the training, and by this time the dog should know that word means 'ignore everything and don't chase anything'.

It is in all these cases the attitude of the owner that matters.

Occasionally I discover the owner is neurotic, and rather enjoys her dog disliking her husband's dog, though she won't admit it. More troubles with dogs are caused because they are mirroring inhibitions with idiosyncrasies of their owners than we know about. That is why it is very difficult for me to diagnose what is wrong with a dog or owner when I only have a letter to read. Although in the end one becomes like a psychologist and quickly sees under the veneer put on for one's benefit.

Over-possessiveness on the part of the owner causes many dogs to do naughty things. The owner who never lets her dog romp with another for fear of picking up something, or the dog that is never allowed a good race over the fields because it gets its newly sham-pooed self dirty, is asking for trouble. Even toy dogs like Yorkshire terriers or pekinese love a rat hunt. A dog becomes a dull creature with nothing but town walks and chauffeur-driven rides in the park. In my school, when the weather permits, we take all the so-called problem dogs into a field, and in spite of protests from owners who feel certain their dogs will fight or get eaten alive, or won't come when called, we let the whole lot go free at the same time. So far we have never had anything terrible happen. Sometimes a fight is immi-nent, but my voice can usually avert it, and soon the owners become confident and willing to trust their dogs, and that is the first step towards a happy dog and owner relationship. Good behavior is undoubtedly infectious, and it is quite amazing to see how good these 'difficult dogs' are in school. If only one could instil the methods of control sufficiently into the owners they would be no trouble at home either. I think lack of time is the main enemy. Practice makes perfect. Working dogs only once a week is useless.

It is the most difficult thing to impress on owners of fighting dogs that to cure them they must have long loose leads, that holding a dog on a short lead tends to make it want to fight more. As they approach a strange dog they must be given a terrific jerk with the command 'Leave', and then the lead must be loose again. A four-foot lead is essential, and a completely indestructible clip. The scissor hook and ordinary hook are dangerous, as both can open with a sharp jerk. Most pet stores will have the strong clip if your market does not. For if a fighting dog did get free when jerked hard it would be twenty times worse than before, because the jerk would have sent it forward when the clip broke and would probably catapult it into the other dog. The jerks to cure fighting dogs must be hard and effective. And above all the owner must learn to trust her dog, otherwise there is no hope of a cure. Some dogs, like Kerry Blues, are born fighters, and although I have cured them I feel a fighting one is an unsuitable pet for a woman unless trained when fairly young.

I think dog owners can be rash in the breed of dog they choose. I wish they would find out more about what the dogs were originally bred for, before they buy one. All the bull-breeds were for fighting in one way or another, also the Irish terriers and Kerry Blues. Why do weak little owners want this type of dog? Is it that they lack courage in their make-up and buy a courageous dog to make up for it?

If you are a flat dweller choose a dog that needs little exercise or work like the King Charles spaniel, whose ancestors are so often pictured in old oil paintings and whose lives in various courts of royalty were well known.

I have met a family who expected a beagle to lead this sort of life and who complained when it became unmanageable. One beagle in a family of children must be a misfit, they are hunting dogs, not playthings, and they have very stubborn natures. The choice of dog must of course rest with the buyer, but I do feel breeders could refuse to sell an old lady a bloodhound, or a small child a big boisterous breed. I suppose those who breed dogs do so for profit, and few can afford to refuse a sale. I only wish they had the dogs to deal with when they become problem dogs, and it would then deter them from selling unsuitable dogs.

If I had my way no dog licences would be granted without the owner passing a simple examination in the care and training of the dog. I suppose so many would fail that it would be impracticable. I never understand why the training of dogs should be considered to be quite easy, and that it is unnecessary to learn anything about it. Few young mothers would have a baby without buying a book and learning about its care, yet owners buy a puppy, and make no effort to learn how to train it, until it becomes a trouble in one way or another. Although I do think that with the help of TV and books the idea is catching on that you must learn yourself what to do if you want an obedient dog.

BEAUTY BATTLES

Oh, the battles that are fought with dogs that don't want to be brushed, or combed, or bathed. And in most cases I sympathize wholeheartedly with the dog. Have you ever had your tangled hair combed with a steel comb? Believe me it hurts. Have you ever been threatened with being put into a bath? It is frightening. Well, thoughtless owners do similar things with dogs and expect them without previous training to put up with them without protesting.

Let's take the brushing and combing first of all. Let's examine what sort of brush and comb you are going to use on your particular type of dog. Poodles seem to be the big offenders in the order of biters when brushed. The reason is obvious: they have a thick tangled coat, or else they are clipped nearly bare, yet never have I seen anyone change their brushes and combs for the different coat conditions. When it has little between it and the brush a poodle gets brushed with a long bristle brush, its ears and feet get combed with a steel comb which has extremely sharp teeth, and I can assure you the dog puts up with considerable discomfort before this operation is completed. It could be done by much kinder methods. If you dog has a tangled coat or ears, damp them and the tangles will come out far more gently. Using a brush with wire mesh, not nylon, the tangles come out easily. Having made certain that no undue discomfort or pain is causing your dog to resist his grooming, go to it in a quiet firm manner, praising him if he stands still, and if he moves or attempts to bite, hold him firmly by the choke chain behind his ears and continue grooming, for if held aloft his head cannot turn to bite you. But of course this only applies to small dogs. Big dogs cannot be held in one hand, and must if necessary be muzzled. Fear on the part of the owner is mostly at the root of these grooming battles, fear of being bitten. Quite naturally so, for a whirling spaniel can bite quickly and deeply when one hand is mixed up with a comb. One method of grooming the body without danger to oneself is to have a big leather collar like those vets use for skin diseases. A dog wearing one of these cannot turn round and bite. But if the grooming is done gently with the right type of brush, and the realization that some dogs are more sensitive to pain than others, there should be no fighting against it at all. I think people with short-coated dogs often groom them too much. I believe that a regular bath to get rid of the old hair and once-a-week good brush with a glove brush is all that short-coated dogs need if kept in the house. Naturally dogs that come in dirty and muddy need more attention. This brings me to the question of baths. Many dogs fight like tigers rather than go into water and have a bath. Why fight them? Surely the ordinary hose type of water spray as used for human beings in hairdressers' makes bathing quite simple. All you have to do is stand the dog in a dry sink and let the water run over him and down the drain. The dog is not frightened, the shampooing can be done quickly, and no one gets hurt. In summer the dog can probably stand outside the kitchen window, and be bathed on the ground with a long hose attached to the spray. I often think owners fight their dogs unnecessarily. I have many dogs brought to me who won't be groomed, and I never have any trouble at all, simply because I am not frightened of being bitten. If I really thought I was going to be bitten I should wear gloves, but so far I have never had to. I don't believe all long-haired dogs enjoy being brushed; I think they tolerate it. I think short-haired dogs do like a glove brush especially under their chests and tummies, but I am appalled at the average weapon I see used for grooming, it is far too harsh. If I owned a spaniel I would keep its ears clipped fairly free of hair unless I had much time to brush them, for they get very tangled and this is one reason why so many spaniel owners complain that their dogs bite them. I know this cannot be done to show dogs, but they get professionally groomed so they don't come into this book. Few people really have time to spend brushing and combing their dogs if they are housewives and mothers, and therefore a trim with the scissors saves a multitude of frictions between dog and owner.

I think dogs are frightened of slipping in their baths. I always used to put a rubber mat on the bottom of the bath to prevent this, and now my dog is accustomed to being bathed and jumps in by herself without fear. I think it is a tip worth taking with big dogs: their nails are so long, they slip easily.

The bathing of dogs could be reduced considerably if only dogs had their faces and under the tail washed with a flannel more often. I am often made to feel quite sick by the smell of some dogs brought to my classes. It is usually caused by the fluid in the anal glands under the tail which secrete a very horrible-smelling liquid, and when this is discharged it makes the dog smell badly. The dog then may lick itself and its nose will smell equally unpleasant. The cure is to make certain the anal glands are kept in their normal condition by either squeezing them yourself, if you know how, or getting the vet to do it when the dog smells excessively, or is seen dragging its bottom along the floor. In the olden days this was said to be worms, but it is much more likely to be enlarged anal glands. In some cases they get painfully enlarged and an operation for their removal has to be done.

A golden rule with biting and resisting dogs who object to beauty treatment is only to do what is essential, do it kindly but firmly, never allowing the dog to win by biting. If it really tries to bite, suspend it for a second off its front legs; it will soon stop that nonsense as its choke chain would make it breathless. Daily gentle grooming and training soon shows results, if not, muzzle it and be finished with the grooming as quickly as possible.

WHAT TO EXPECT FROM DOGS

I feel no chapter on 'Difficult Dogs' would be complete without some mention of how much we can expect from our dogs. Sometimes I get letters that make me wonder if owners believe six-month-old dogs, or rather puppies, should behave exactly like adult dogs. That they should never bark or whine, or tear things up, or have fits of temper, or refuse to come when called. It is quite possible to achieve this, providing the owner gives up enough time to training the puppy as soon as it leaves the nest and enters its new home. I well remember our little English toy terrier giving a demonstration with my daughter of nine years old when the puppy was only ten weeks old. This she did in front of 2,000 children at an Odeon cinema with strange lights and noisy children. The little dog could hardly be seen as she only weighed four pounds, nevertheless she did the full schedule of 'Special Beginners' including retrieving a dumb-bell that was nearly as big as herself. She did it all with complete confidence and apparently enjoyed herself. But it does not mean that the little dog never did anything wrong. She did. She was naughty about barking too long when strangers came to the door, she sometimes ran off with the children's slippers, and stole food from the chicken bucket. But that was what I expected. A dog that had none of the naughty puppy sins in my opinion would be cowed or have little spirit. Many people recommend that no puppy should even begin its training until it is six months old. I say that's wrong. I recommend that all puppies should start at about three months old, immediately after they have received their last shots from the vet, which gives them protection against hard pad and distemper. For to train a dog properly in all it should do it must mix with people and other dogs, and no puppy should risk this until it is immunized. Then the puppy should have short daily training in walking to heel, lying down, and coming when called. I never worry much about the 'sit' exercise in young puppies as they tire so soon. If they learn to sit when doing heel work that is all that matters, just a very temporary sit. They can be taught to carry a rolled-up glove or stocking and be made to give it up easily, which will prevent future battles over bones that they mustn't have. Never try and pull anything out of a dog's mouth. You won't get it easily. Just give a quick downward jerk and the dog must give it up. A slow jerk won't do it. I have often taught puppies to give things up by having a little meat in one hand and when I want the object the pup has got, I say 'Give' and put the meat near his nose. The object is dropped, and he gets the meat. Very soon he connects dropping the object with the word 'give' and a nice titbit. Again pleasant association of ideas helps enormously with young dogs—or for that matter with any dog.

I do not think that when a puppy is out for a walk you can expect him all at once to give up smelling that most intriguing smell and immediately come to heel. Give him a little licence—after all his life is full of scents and exciting smells at first. But never for one second must he run away when you call him, or his life may be in danger from traffic. If he does that he must be put on a long cord and given a very quick jerk as he runs away. If done on soft grass he will not harm himself at all, and the shock of going the way he never intended soon teaches him to listen for his owner's 'Come'.

I think one of the most important things in aiding training is to give a dog a sensible name. So many dogs come to my classes with names that can hardly be said, let alone called out. Too soft a sounding name carries badly; so does a too complicated one. The name should carry a long way when the dog is called, so keep this in mind when naming a dog.

That is also why you must always use single words of command in calling a dog or for that matter giving any command. For example, 'Here, old chap,' will not bring the dog as quickly as 'Peter, come'. In the first place the name has been left out and secondly 'here' does not carry as well as the harder sounding word 'come'. Some people use the word 'flat' to put their dogs down. It is not a good word. The word 'down', with its rounded intonation, carries much farther. Similarly you should never say 'Heel, Peter'. It should always be 'Peter, heel'. Then his wandering attention is brought back before he hears the order to be obeyed.

I think by the time the dog is ten to twelve months old, if it has had regular or daily training, it should be perfectly reliable in all things. I don't believe it takes two years or even one year to train a dog. Naturally it depends on the dog and the ability of the owner, but I feel that if a dog hasn't reached a pretty high standard by twelve months, the owner should look to his or her training of the dog and try and learn a little more about this fascinating subject.

When I say a high standard, I am not referring to obedience work as found in the show rings today. I couldn't care less about that for the ordinary dog. What I mean is the dog should have learnt to stay quietly alone at home or in the car; should come reasonably quickly when called; should ignore other dogs when on the lead and if given the command 'Leave' when out walking; should be house trained, and should not chase anything unless allowed to, and should certainly not be destructive.

If you wish to reach the heights of obedience in the show ring it may take you years to reach the top. You should if possible join a club where this type of enthusiast reigns supreme, and you must want to win terribly, and in my opinion you needn't love your dog too well, for undoubtedly it is a form of torment for some dogs, to do over and over again these pretty useless gyrations. I have done it, so I know what dogs feel about it and I am positive few enjoy it for very long, if ever. The owners are nervous, or angry when things go wrong. They may not praise their dogs in the ring, and they may not even behave naturally. But it is a sport, and dogs have been used in sport for centuries. I don't expect greyhounds like never catching the hare.

I believe that training should last only until the dog has become sociable, obedient and friendly. After that it almost becomes a disease and has little fun in it for the dog. After all, army dogs and police dogs do occasionally catch a criminal. Ordinary show obedience dogs get little else but praise from their owners, and very often more jerks than praise. Naturally I think anything that spreads the gospel that it is quite easy to train a dog is a good thing, and when thousands of people watch obedience work at shows I am quite sure some go home and try it out for themselves and get interested enough to train their own dog.

DOG'S EYE VIEW OF OWNERS

I would very much like to hear what some dogs think of their owners. I have a horrid suspicion it would not be too complimentary. What do we owe to our dogs? I think quite a lot. I think as household pets they bring enormous pleasure and comfort and companionship into the lives of millions. Apart from household pets, dogs cause millions of pounds to change hands, and bring to this country much-needed dollars. They make friends for their owners in different countries all over the world. And entertain millions of people on the race track, the show ring and the circus, TV, and the entertainment halls. We as a world owe dogs a lot. They give employment to countless hundreds of people who produce dog biscuits and merchandise of all kinds. They give vets plenty of work.

They give interesting employment to kennel maids, hunt servants, and occasionally even to Embassy officials, I am told. They give love and pleasure to the lowest and highest in our land and all over the world. Yet they have no control over their destiny, and we, their masters or mistresses, can make their lives heaven or hell.

Nowadays more and more people are striving to learn more about training their canine friends, so that they will remain their friends. Very many dogs are not repaying this care and love given to them by their owners. Why is this? I think the main reason is that owners forget dogs are dogs, they treat them like human beings and expect them to behave that way. We all know that by training a dog can reach a very high standard of intelligence. My own dog has been described as 'almost human' by the press hundreds of times, yet nobody has yet called her or any other dog 'human', only 'almost human'. If the owner is willing to understand this slight difference she will be fair to her dog.

I think a dog can expect from its owner that in all her dealings with the dog she should control her temper. The dog gets bewildered by a lost temper, and no dog has even benefited by one.

I think also that the dog may reasonably expect the owner to know what she really wants the dog to do, and that when she gives an order she will be concentrating with her mind as well as her voice. A dog quickly gets muddled if the owner gives a command, but her mind is thinking 'Poor little chap, how he hates doing it'. If she feels that way about it, why train the dog? Her attitude is really one of sympathy in case the dog fails the exercise instead of desire to make him do it well.

The dog can hope also that the owner makes him do things for some sensible reason and not just to flatter her vanity, or show off to friends.

Dogs may surely hope that their owners will occasionally let them have a good rough and tumble with the stray dogs they meet on the common. Those dogs often have something very vital and exciting about them, and a game with them is far more fun than with Mrs. Binks's perfumed poodle.

I feel very strongly that a dog has a right to be taken on holiday with its owner, and not left behind with strangers whilst she enjoys herself. Dogs enjoy a change of air and scenery too. A trained dog devoted to its owner suffers tortures when left behind, however kind the boarding kennels, unless it is the fickle don't-care type of dog, and they never train very well anyway.

Dogs love their owners with all their faults; they don't care whether they are ugly, tall or small, rich or poor. I wish owners felt the same about their dogs. Dogs suffer a lot of misery when owners criticize them in front of friends. They know the apologetic tone of voice used when an owner is telling someone her dog would be good if it didn't have bad ear carriage or some such nonsense. The tone of voice depresses the dog, although it doesn't understand why. So don't pull your dog to pieces in front of it.

A dog thinks the owner wonderful if she thinks it wonderful. I always tell owners who come to my school to believe their dogs are good and good they will be. If you think your dog is going to run away or fight it probably will; faith in your dog's goodness is picked up by the dog and it reacts accordingly.

And lastly a dog has the right to hope that if it is not wanted any more its owner will have mercy enough to put it to sleep, and thus make sure it has a happy end. So many owners lack the moral courage to do this for their pets, and give quite middle-aged dogs away to so-called kind homes rather than face up to their responsibility. Some young dogs can be given new homes and be happy. Very few old dogs can. They get set in their ways just like human beings. If they have had a good kind loving owner, they have got used to her ways of life, and may not behave so well in a new home. I think it is kinder to put them to sleep.

CHASING CARS

Dogs that chase moving things are a menace and must be cured at all costs. Car-chasing is one of their worst crimes. When I was in Ireland recently I noticed all the dogs in country districts chased cars. Nobody seemed to do anything about it, and the dogs were incredibly clever at avoiding getting run over. I am glad to say the dogs in Great Britain that chase cars are the exception rather than the rule. But when they do get this dangerous habit they undoubtedly cause many accidents. How can it be stopped? The quickest and most efficient way I know is to enlist the aid of a friend with a car. Ask him to drive you slowly past the dog that chases cars, and as the dog comes in to the attack throw out as hard as you possibly can any fat hard-covered book, and make certain that the book hits the dog. The shock it gives the dog so frightens it that I have never had to repeat the treatment more than twice, even though the dog may have chased cars for years. My favourite book is an old A.A. Handbook, it is just the right size. Try not to lean out of the car to throw it as then the dog may connect you with the throwing of the book, when you want him to connect the car with the shock he gets.

If the dog has only just developed the car or motor-bike chasing vice, a long cord on a choke chain and a terrific jerk as he goes to chase the vehicle works a cure, but an old hand at the game knows when he is on the cord and won't do it. Shepherds always say a sheep chaser is quickly taught to leave sheep alone by being penned with a fierce ram, and chicken chasers with a turkey cock, but I wouldn't like to bet on that.

I have in an earlier part of this book gone fully into the cure of chicken chasers, so I will not discuss that here. But I hope the owners of car-chasing dogs will try the book-throwing cure and let me know the result. I have found it far superior to any other cure for bicycle chasers too. The old idea of giving the dog a kick was always stupid and cruel I thought. For one thing the dog quickly learnt to avoid the kick as the Irish dogs learnt to avoid being hit by a car. But a book thrown with skill can reach the dog every time, and frighten it without the risk of injuring it.

I recently cured a corgi that chased motor-cycles by getting the motor-cyclist to carry a jug of water in one hand and throw it over the dog as she came in to chase the motor-cycle. It took three dousings to cure her, but now she shrinks back into the ditch at the approach of a motor-cycle, and this may well have saved her life.

All chasing of vehicles and livestock can be stopped by proper training in the recall exercise. A dog should never be so far away from its owner that it cannot be recalled. No dog should be off the lead on the highway these days, there is too much traffic. If the dog shows the least excitement at the approach of a vehicle it should be given a sharp jerk and the command 'Leave'.

No dog should ever be free where there are livestock unless the owner is absolutely certain his dog will stay to heel. Far too many owners look upon farmers' fields as their natural right of way and allow their dogs to wander out of hearing before they attempt to call them in to heel. If the dog is constantly taken amongst traffic and livestock on the lead the novelty soon wears off and the chasing does not occur. If only owners would think ahead and be alive to the risk that their dog may chase livestock, I feel sure it would never happen.

The fact remains that many people encourage their dogs to chase things, and the poor dog has to learn what he can chase and what he can't. Some dogs drive their owners mad by chasing birds on the lawn, some by running up and down the garden fence when people or dogs or vehicles go by. What is the cure? Keep the dog in away from temptation. I find a vast number of people whose dogs have many vices prefer to grumble rather than remove the source of vice. They obviously haven't the skill to train their dogs, so they must do the next best thing and keep the dog out of the way of temptation. Take for example the bitch that destroys everything in the house. Surely the best way to stop it is to confine her when you are not about in an indoor kennel lined with zinc. She can then do no damage. If she never has a chance to destroy things she forgets the vice, and it is a good bet that she will have grown tired of doing it when she is again given the run of the house.

Some bitches nine weeks or so after their heat make nests and tear things up as a result of pseudo-pregnancy. They imagine they are going to have puppies and prepare a nest accordingly. Many people do not seem to realize what is going on and merely put these actions down to vice and lack of training. I wish someone in the veterinary world would find a satisfactory cure for this curious phenomenon. I have tried hormone treatment without the slightest effect. And whilst I am on this strange period in a bitch's life, I have noticed time and time again that this is also the time when they suffer from a mild form of metritis, or inflammation of the womb, and with my own bitch I always put her on a course of antibiotics for a few days. She soon returns to her normal self, whereas formerly she would drag about after me and be very dull. I don't wait for trouble now. I treat as soon as her heat is over. This is not a training hint, but obedience training fans have often found their dogs work badly after their heat period, and this tip might help them get their dogs in first-class working order again.

I honestly believe some dogs that chase things and tear things up have a mental disease. If firm training does not stop them, and giving them plenty of interest in life has no effect, then I think there is no cure. I knew one fox terrier who used to chase his own tail like mad every morning. On his death he was found to have a tumour on the brain. There are 'mental' human beings and 'mental' dogs. Training must not be condemned as useless until the possibility of a mental disease in the dog has been eliminated, for however good you are at training dogs, a dog with a diseased brain will never respond.

I meet many people who have sent their dogs away to be trained, or who have attended training clubs, without apparent improvement in their dogs. They go around saying obedience training is no good. This is not the case. Not everyone who starts a training club is qualified to train problem dogs. Most of those clubs are run by dog lovers with a certain amount of experience, and are doing a very good job helping people with normal dogs to get a better-behaved animal. Those who expect to send a dog away and get it returned obedient to their every wish in my humble opinion are expecting too much, for it is the owner who must be trained. I know people who send their dogs to keepers to be trained. The dog gives its affection to the keeper and is miserable when it returns. The right person to train the dog is the owner. Others can help but the owner must do the job.

SOME CAUSES OF BAD DOGS

Finally I think many people before dubbing their dog a bad dog would be wise to consult a vet or someone who thoroughly under- stands dogs, to find out whether there is some physical reason for the dog's bad behaviour before attempting to train him. For example many dogs are deaf without their owners knowing it. This may be caused by canker, or by some inherited factor. Make sure that your dog does hear you when you call him before labelling him a 'difficult dog'.

Pain in the ear can cause a dog to snap without warning: he is frightened you are going to hurt him. Many people clean inside their dog's ears as a routine, thus causing the dog's eardrum to become inflamed. Ears should only be wiped clean on the external parts, it is extremely dangerous to try to clean the delicate inside. Ear drops will do anything that is necessary without poking with your finger, which is far too thick to be safe.

Grooming a dog with painful ears can cause the dog much pain, so do you wonder that he bites to protect himself?

Sometimes injections by the vet can leave residual painful swelling which the owner doesn't notice, and the dog bites when you touch his shoulder perhaps. Make sure this isn't the case before you decide that your dog is vicious.

Dogs get headaches and have off days like human beings. Be certain your dog is quite well before condemning him as stubborn when he doesn't obey you quickly. If he has a cold nose and no temperature you can be reasonably sure that the dog is in good health, providing he has not diarrhoea. But always go by the look in his eye; a dull eye means something is wrong. A too sleepy dog usually indicates indigestion, and no dog works well with indigestion. Be sure his diet is right, and he gets plenty of raw meat, for that is a dog's natural and best diet.

Bitches behave queerly for some weeks after their heat, and with greyhounds they may not race for three months. Give your bitch a chance to recover before you blame her too much for erratic behav- iour. Dogs living within the proximity of bitches on heat never concentrate. Remember nature governs nearly all their actions and don't expect good concentration if their minds are on the lady friend next door.

Remember a puppy tires easily and can concentrate for only a short time: keep the lesson short and interesting and have a game with the puppy between exercises to hold his interest, for a bored puppy is a bad worker. Old dogs tire quickly and their lessons should be short too.

You yourself must be feeling fine and well to work a dog. It is a tiring occupation, and if your mind or body is tired you will not make a good trainer. Five minutes when you feel well is worth fifty-five when you have a headache. If you feel irritable don't train your dog. You must love dogs terribly to get good results, and by loving dogs I don't mean being sloppy and sentimental, I mean being at all times fair to them and being willing to give up a lot for them, including them in your family circle, with practically the same rights as the children.

A well-trained dog is worth its weight in gold: it is up to you to see you are a well-trained owner.

Epilogue

This book would not be complete without a word or two on what I feel about the different breeds of dogs. So many peeple ask me what kind they should have, wishing to be certain that they can train them easily. The answer is bound to be vague, for my advice is: choose whatever dog you fancy, for it will be the one you fancy that is the easiest for you to train. If you are persuaded to have what you don't really want, any faults will be blamed on the breed. Try not to have a dog beyond your strength, try not to have a very sporting breed in town, but whatever you choose he will be yours to do with as you will, and therefore precious and perfect in your eyes. And that is how it should be. Love is a queer thing. I know owners whose lives are made a misery by the dogs they own, but as they love them they will put up with endless discomfort and sometimes injury for the sake of their brown-eyed stealer of hearts. Most dog owners who really love their dogs feel the death of their pals as grievously as that of one of the family. When I lost my favourite Alsatian I could not bring myself to own a dog for ten years; he was irreplaceable. Once a dog has entwined himself round your heart he is not only yours for life, but you are his. When he is gone, his place is for ever sacred. Other dogs are just as precious but they all have their allotted spot in your affections kept for them or their memory. A heaven without one's dogs would not be the heaven we hope for. A dog is always man's best friend.